Since I raised boys exclusively, I appreciated the insights Patricia gives in this book regarding their training, and hope that many future *wives* will benefit from marrying a man whose mom applied the principles of this book.

My feelings are that the softer moms make it for their kids the harder it is for them to make a balanced entry into the real world, and Patricia keenly delineates this principle.

This book will be more than a "read it once and stick it on the shelf" book. I think it will be more like a daily manual for parents who struggle with the task of exhorting their children to become responsible adults.

Barbara Johnson
Author of *Stick a Geranium in Your Hat and Be Happy*
and *Splashes of Joy in the Cesspools of Life*

This is one of the best books I have ever read explaining why chores are mandatory and then how to incorporate them into the child's routine. Patricia Sprinkle has done an excellent job of giving us the "how to's" of raising a responsible child.

Robert G. Barnes, Ed.D.
Executive Director, Sheridan House Family Ministries
Author of *Raising Confident Kids*

Kids *need* to do chores, and Patricia Sprinkle does a great job of showing parents how to get them involved. I'm putting this book on my recommended reading list for parents I counsel.

Andy Bustanoby
Marriage and Family Therapist
Author of *Single Parenting*
and *Tough Parenting for Dangerous Times* (with Verne Becker)

Children who work feel needed; those who don't are cheated.

Bonnie McCullough
Coauthor, 401 *Ways to Get Your Kids to Work*
and *Totally Organized*

As Mark Twain said of the weather, "Everybody's talking about it, but nobody's doing anything about it." That's the way with children and chores around the house. Here is a book of suggestions on how to bring about changes in behavior. Parents will find help and understanding as well.

Jay Kesler
President, Taylor University

I am a great believer in helping children to be self-sufficient. I think we do far too much for children in our western world as it is. Patricia Sprinkle's book therefore is a breath of fresh air. It touches on a critical aspect of parenting that I think is totally neglected these days. All parents, as well as teachers, will find the book a helpful resource in teaching self-sufficiency.

Archibald D. Hart, Ph.D.
Dean and professor of psychology,
Fuller Theological Seminary

CHILDREN WHO DO TOO LITTLE

Why Your Kids Need to Work Around the House
(and How to Get Them to Do It)

Previously titled *Do I Have To?*

Patricia H. Sprinkle

ZondervanPublishingHouse
Grand Rapids, Michigan

A Division of HarperCollinsPublishers

Children Who Do Too Little
Copyright © 1993, 1996 by Patricia H. Sprinkle

Previously titled *Do I Have To?*

Requests for information should be addressed to:

▦ ZondervanPublishingHouse
Grand Rapids, Michigan 49530

Library of Congress Cataloging-in-Publication Data

Sprinkle, Patricia Houck.
   [Do I have to?]
   Children who do too little : why your kids need to work around the house
(and how to get them to do it) / Patricia H. Sprinkle.
     p.   cm.
   Originally published: Do I have to? c1993.
   Includes bibliographical references.
   ISBN: 0-310-21146-8 (softcover)
   1. Work.   2. Child development.   3. Work ethic.   4. Child rearing.
I. Title.
[HQ784.W6S67   1996]
649'.1—dc 20   96–14879
                                                CIP

Printed in the United States of America

---

97 98 99 00 01 02 /DH/ 10 9 8 7 6 5 4

For Barnabas and David,
with love and thanks for all they do

CONTENTS

Preface

M Y F R I E N D John, age twelve, assures me that this book will make me rich. "Parents will buy it, kids will burn it, parents will buy another one, the kids will burn that one"—deep sigh—"but by that time it'll be too late. The parents will've already read it."

This, you see, is a book about children and housework. It talks about why children desperately need to learn household skills, what we can realistically expect from them at various ages, why we often don't teach them the skills they need to know, and how we may have to change ourselves in order to help them become all God intends them to be.

I wrote this book not out of great expertise but out of my own need to know. When my sons—now fifteen and twelve—were born, I found many books about how, when, and what to feed them, but nothing on when and how to start them cooking and washing dishes. Experts told me when to toilet train them but were strangely silent about when to train them to *clean* the toilets.

Since my husband and I started our family later in our lives, I got to watch my peers raise older children. I benefited greatly from their wisdom but have been increasingly disturbed that we modern parents seem to do a great deal *for* our young and expect very little *from* them—and that, as they enter adulthood, so many modern children seem unwilling or even unable to function on their own.

When I interviewed women for *Women Who Do Too Much: Stress and the Myth of the Superwoman* (Zondervan, 1990), some mothers said their stress was in part due to enormous amounts of time they spent caring for their children, cleaning up after them, and driving them to a myriad of activities. Few mothers expected the children to reciprocate. Several women whose children were already grown, however, said things like, "I wish I had expected more from them when they were at home. It would have made things easier for all of us, and it would have taught them what they now need to know to live on their own."

Spurred by their regrets and a suspicion that children, like adults, need to be contributing parts of society, I started talking to educators, personnel directors, and family counselors. I interviewed parents who have raised or currently are raising responsible children. I also talked to some of their adult children. Most of the wisdom in these pages isn't mine but was gleaned from others' experiences. Appendix A contains short biographical sketches of people whose names I use.

I'm now convinced that when we don't involve children in regular household tasks, we do a great disservice to the children, to our families, and to society as a whole. If we fail to teach a child to take care of personal needs and to function responsibly as part of a family team, we may be raising a child with limited capacity for holding down a job, sustaining a healthy marriage, or ministering to others. To put it bluntly, *children who do too little in childhood may not grow up capable of doing enough as adults.*

I'm also convinced that we as parents do ourselves a disservice if we carry the full load of regular household chores and fail to share them with our children.

I wish I had known when our sons were young what I now know and share in this book. One thing I've learned, however, is that it's *never* too late to begin. Even a young adult newly arrived back at home can be placed in a "school for adulthood" and expected to function as part of a family team instead of an honored guest.

May our perfect heavenly Parent sustain all of us imperfect earthly parents as we seek to turn our fledglings into adults equipped to live in and be responsible for the world. I pray that you will find encouragement and ideas here to help you in the process. You may find you also lighten your own load along the way. And when your child sticks out that lower lip and demands, "Do I have to?" this book will give you plenty of ammunition to reply, firmly and confidently, "You most certainly do!"

PART ONE

Why Children Need to Work

CHAPTER ONE

Mockingbirds Don't Stroll, Honey

WHEN THE DISHWASHER BROKE, a woman left a note for her teenage son to find after school: "Please wash the dishes in the sink before your father gets home." The woman got a call at work. "Mom, I can't wash dishes. The dishwasher's broken."

That's a true story. Every family has at least one like it. There's the mother who, on learning that her daughter was admitted to Yale, exclaimed, "This child can't even sort laundry! I've got nine months to teach her everything she really needs to know." Or the mother whose dinner party was interrupted by a married daughter calling long distance: "What do you put with chicken to make a nutritious meal?" Or the first-year college student who got up her first morning in the dorm, put coffee in the top of her brand-new coffee maker, put water in the pot beneath it, and waited for it to brew.

We chuckle at those stories. As parents, however, we also may wonder, "Will *my* children know what they need to know when they grow up? Am I teaching them everything they need to learn?"

But it's so *hard* to teach them! They complain. We lose our tempers. They have so much to do. We have so much to do. Why bother to teach household skills when it's such a hassle for everyone?

Early one spring morning I carried a mug of tea out to our porch for a time of peace and prayer before starting work. We are blessed to live on a quiet street with a landscaped median and small stream, so that even in the city I have a view of flowers and trees from my rocker. That particular morning I was admiring white sprays of bridal wreath when a small mockingbird came strolling down our sidewalk. Behind him trotted a wise and determined mother.

She ran up and butted him gently. He picked up his pace. She butted him harder. He ran faster.

She backed up, rushed down the sidewalk, and butted him so hard he was pitched into the air. He fluttered his wings a few times—and headed for a convenient crape myrtle.

Landing on a nearby branch, she gave him a good piece of her mind. Then she shoved him out.

He flew back to the sidewalk—and resumed his stroll.

That mockingbird mother got mad! Squawking at the top of her lungs, she flew down and hit him in the backside with a tail-jolting thud that propelled him a good four feet off the ground! Convinced, the little bird finally flew.

That mockingbird mother knew something her child had not yet learned: strolling mockingbirds don't survive.

A WISE PARENT KNOWS:
The ultimate purpose of parenting is to help our children move out of our lives.

Are we human parents as wise as mockingbirds? We provide our children with education, religious training, security, vaccinations, and the four food groups. Do we also teach them practical life skills they may literally need to survive?

Parenting is a more demanding role than most of us know when we sign on for it. One Sunday a new father stood up in church and confessed, "Having a baby is humbling me. I never knew how self-centered I was! I have to feed her before I feed myself, walk the floor when I'd rather sleep, and change a dirty diaper when I'd rather wait for my wife to come home and do it." He held the infant close. "I thank God babies cry. When she cries, she forces me to put her needs before my own."

As children mature, however, what they cry for and what they need are often very different. It is up to us parents to know what they really need—and be willing to meet those needs, even when it requires a sacrifice of our time or sometimes even of "the way I am."

Dorothy, mother of two young teens, said, "I think today's parents need to stand up and take control of their children. In some of my children's friends' homes, the children are in charge. The parents spend all their time trying to make the children happy: carting them from one place to another, never asking them to do anything around the house. But it's up to us to teach our children to become independent and self-sufficient adults. They may not feel they need to know these things, but it is our responsibility to teach them, whether or not they want to learn."

Let's consider several good reasons why we need to teach them to work.

THE NEED TO CARE FOR ONESELF

Don't you love novels in which families have a cook, two maids, a gardener, a chauffeur, and a nanny who brings well-scrubbed children in for afternoon tea? My husband sometimes teases me that that was what I expected from marriage. Alas, I haven't gotten it yet!

Life won't ever be like that for most of us, but children waited on hand and foot by their parents may believe it will. "My son is growing up thinking somebody will always be around to pick up his dirty clothes," one father admitted.

An army recruiter shakes his head. "You have to teach the new recruits *everything* these days. They can't make a bed, polish their shoes, scarcely wipe their own noses."

In this era of velcro shoes, microwave ovens, dishwashers, pocket calculators, and computer spellcheck programs, children—and many parents!—may not see the need to teach simple skills like how to tie a knot, how to cook and wash dishes when the power goes off, how to add up a family's income and subtract what has been spent.

One study of six hundred children in first grade through seventh grade reported that four out of five children said they had regular chores. A careful reader of the data, however, wonders what chores the children were given. Barely half (53 percent) of seventh graders were expected to help with housework. Only 52 percent were expected to clean their own room. Less than 33 percent ever did dishes or yardwork, and fewer than 20 percent helped with cooking, ran errands, or set the table. In fact, very little more was expected from seventh graders than from third graders, except that a few seventh graders did yardwork.[1]

Yet how—except by doing—can a child learn to plan and cook balanced meals, clean up afterward, buy and maintain clothing, or keep a house and yard?

A WISE PARENT KNOWS:
The only way to learn the rules
of anything practical
is to begin to do the thing.

George MacDonald

Strangely enough, children are born wanting to take care of their own needs. What parent hasn't had a toddler grab a spoon and insist, "Me do it!" Most two-year-olds would rather wear shoes on the wrong feet than let you put them on, would rather go out with hair standing on end than let you brush it.

Given that strong urge in small children to manage their own lives, how do we currently end up with so many young adults who can't? It would be interesting someday to study just when and how the desire to do for oneself gets transformed into a desire to be done for. Does it begin the fifth time the parent insists on putting on the child's shoes to get somewhere on time? The tenth time the parent insists on feeding the child because it's neater?

The end result may not be neater. One couple left an eighteen-year-old alone at home for six weeks. They returned to find the sink full of dishes and dirty clothes strewn from the back door across the kitchen and down the hall to his room. The son had actually gone shopping for new jeans because he had no clean ones!

Where did today's *parents* learn (or fail to learn) to clean, cook, do laundry, manage money, and manage a home? Probably from our parents, grandparents, or a home economics teacher. Today most grandparents live too far away to do much household training, and home economics classes have been demoted to six weeks in middle school. High school curricula are too full of advanced math and science to require courses in household skills.

Who is left to teach children practical life skills? Only busy, involved parents, who have so much else to do.

It may comfort you to know that young children don't mind learning to work. One survey of 250 schoolchildren found that 97 percent of the children thought they *ought* to be working at home. Families who expect regular chores from children report they get far less grumbling about those chores than parents who ask a child to do only an occasional job.

Maria Montessori, a pioneer in the field of childhood education, observed that "the adult in our culture is unprepared to recognize and accept the young child's desire for work and, therefore, is not only amazed when it appears, but refuses to allow its expression. He instead tries to force the child to play continuously. Adults must learn to recognize the child's instinct for work and cooperate with it."[2]

THE NEED TO SERVE ON A FAMILY TEAM

When author John Rosemond asked an audience of five hundred people, "How many of you expect your kids to do regular chores for which they are not paid?" perhaps fifty parents raised their hands. When he asked, "How many of your parents expected you to do chores?" almost every hand went up, with laughter.

"This is no laughing matter," he declares. "In the short span of one generation we have managed to misplace a very important tenet of childrearing: children should be *contributing* members of their families."[3]

Dr. Robert Barnes, a family and marriage counselor and director of a home for troubled children, says, "In many homes, parents think making a child do chores is more hassle than it's worth. But once children have learned to do chores, they feel like team members who are working toward the good of the whole family. That makes them more emotionally mature."

In the workplace, time-management experts urge leaders to delegate work for four important reasons:

1. delegation increases effectiveness, because more gets done in less time;
2. delegation releases time for other activities;
3. delegation teaches decision making to those being taught;
4. delegation develops others' skills, initiative, and competence.

Consider those reasons from both a parent's and a child's point of view. Isn't delegation in the home at least as important as it is in business?

Being part of a family team also teaches several important values:

1. *The family is a priority.* One morning while I was working on this book, an abandoned mother of three called me and wept. "It's like a nightmare, living like this! My husband had a good job, but he didn't like it, so he quit. Now he won't pay bills, won't take responsibility for his children. When he left us, he went home to

his mother—and she's taking care of him. She washes his clothes, cooks his meals, even pays his bills. She always has. But who is going to take care of *his* children?"

Some people blame the condition of the modern family on soaring divorce rates. After studying the importance of sharing household responsibilities in a family, I'm beginning to wonder if we don't have it backward. Is it possible that one cause of the soaring divorce rate is the failure of families—whether they have one or two parents—to require children to do their share of the family's work?

Parents often excuse children from household chores because they have so much schoolwork. Robert Barnes said, "Those children are being taught that work is more important than family. As adults they will stay at the office longer hours and neglect their families, because they see themselves only as family providers, not as part of a family team. To assume that children will come out of the house as adults to only do a profession, never housework, is unrealistic. *It is to raise children who are basically unmarriageable.*"

Barbara, an ordained minister and mother of two, agrees. "All of us need to feel we contribute to our families, households, and communities, and doing chores is one way to learn that you are important and your hands are important. You don't contribute just with your brains."

Other children are driven to a myriad of team practices and extracurricular events, dressed in expensive clothes, shipped off to European summer study programs, and generally treated as young royalty. One mother excuses her children from chores because of their homework, ballet, horseback-riding lessons, baseball, basketball, and soccer. "There's so much to do. They're constantly running. I would just like them to grow up well adjusted." Will they be well adjusted to cope with the chores and day-to-day routines of adulthood? Or will they get married expecting to play their way through life while someone else—their marriage partner—takes care of and supports them in the manner to which they have become very accustomed? Only a miracle turns a child raised as a prince or princess into a mature marriage partner.

We parents, therefore, need not only to train our own children but also to pray that their future spouses are being trained to see the family as a team that works together and supports one another.

In my interviews I discovered that families headed by single parents were more likely than others to expect children to function as parts of the family team. "We have to pitch in together," a single father of three told me. "If we didn't, nothing would get done." A delightful thirteen-year-old girl spiced my interview with her single mother with saucy remarks: "Brooke keeps this household live!" "If it weren't for Brooke, this place would fall apart!" "Brooke is Miss Clean!"

2. *Housework belongs to everyone.* While I was writing this book, a friend sent a front-page article from the *Washington Post* reporting on *New Families, No Families,* a 1991 sociological study of "the domestic division of labor."[4] The study reveals something most of us knew already: children are helping out less around the house than they did in the past. What is surprising in the study is that better-educated parents assign fewer household chores to children than less-educated families, even though educated husbands do more chores.

Is something missing in all that education?

"I'm impressed at the extent to which men are moving in," the article quotes Brown University sociologist Frances Goldscheider. "What I found scariest . . . is that it looks like kids are dropping out altogether."

These households seem to place a low value on household tasks. One mother, who runs a catering business, told interviewers, "Knowing how to cook and clean is not a necessity of life." She herself does most of the day-to-day work of running the home in addition to running her business. Why is this mother working so hard?

When I was doing research for *Women Who Do Too Much,* I was struck by the amount of time modern women, even busy professional women, spend maintaining homes. I read several books about relieving women's stress, and most of them suggested ways to do housework more efficiently. None of them suggested another obvious solution: give children regular household tasks.

Before you break into hoots of laughter, I *know* that teaching children to do chores and overseeing them increases stress—in the short run. But I also know that families who work together on a regular basis function more smoothly and eventually put far less stress on one or two members. If my twelve-year-old son were not cooking dinner tonight, I could never finish this chapter on time.

Working on the family team also helps both boys and girls value the work it takes to maintain a home. One study of children and work found that children overwhelmingly dismiss housework as "non-work" because those who perform it don't get paid. They equate "work" with "money." "Women, mothers in particular, headed the children's list of non-workers. . . . As one six-year-old explained, 'not the mommies, just the daddies' worked." The authors concluded, "It is clear that many children do not conceive of being a housewife or mother as 'work.'"[5]

Many fathers also don't know how much work maintaining a household entails. In *Living, Loving, Leading*, David Mains describes humorously how his own eyes were opened when his wife, Karen, went on a six-week mission trip and left him responsible for the house and their four school-age children. "It must have been about a month into my pilgrimage that this new thought came to me: *it seems like what needs to be done today is a lot like what needed to be done yesterday.*"[6]

Today's children are growing up in a world where men and women increasingly share care of the home. A boy who doesn't know how to maintain a house is at a distinct disadvantage. Barnes said, "There are no gender chores. A boy should not grow up thinking, 'I don't have to do this because I am a boy.' In our society, that is a dangerous philosophy."

3. *Serving others is important.* In addition to teaching a child to value family and share the load, serving on the family team is one way a child learns to minister to others. Last evening our younger son wormed his way through a low attic to carry electrical wire for

his father, who is installing a fan in the boys' bathroom. On Sunday his brother cleared the table so his father and I could spend time with a special guest. Children need to learn to care for others, and a family provides many opportunities. Robert Barnes has coined a word to say what happens to children who *aren't* expected to serve within the family: they become "unministryable"—not likely to minister to others spontaneously.

THE NEED TO DEVELOP A WORK ETHIC

The third reason we need to teach our children to work is that children who are given regular jobs at home and expected to do them learn promptness, order, industry, honesty, dependability, and a good attitude toward work. "Work is an extension of personality. It is an achievement. It is one of the ways in which a person defines himself or herself, measures worth and humanity."[7]

Children who don't learn to work as part of a family work team may not be able later to function as part of a corporate work team. "One change I see in today's young adults," says the manager of a personnel firm, "is that they want to know what they will get out of a business—benefits, vacation—but they don't think about or discuss what they have to offer."

A psychologist asked by a state rehabilitation center to treat men considered "unemployable" finds they have one thing in common: none learned to work as a child.

The father of a grown son buries his head in his hands. "I can't get him to leave home. To be honest, he can't hold down a job long enough to earn the money he'd need to live on his own."

As long ago as 1972, the U.S. Secretary for Health, Education, and Welfare commissioned a special task force to study work in America. It was feared that the work ethic was being replaced by a no-work ethic. By 1984, 42 percent of the class of 1980 were still "nesting" under their parents' roof *four years after graduation*! Furthermore, each generation of college students was saving less and spending more than previous generations.[8]

If we ask young adults and their parents why this trend

continues, they give a variety of answers: "Everything is more expensive than it used to be." "You can't make it on today's salaries." "Good jobs are scarce."

Personnel directors, however, tell a different story. "We don't get as good a quality of young employees as we used to," said Donna Clark, owner of Clark Personnel Services. "Some feel this is a place where they can just come and play."

My own observation—that few young adults want to start at the bottom of a career—was echoed by John Richey of the Alabama Power Company, "They aren't as hungry as we were thirty years ago. They come in here expecting to be put in charge right away. They are impatient with the repetitive hard work entailed in learning a job. They want to know, 'Why should I work harder than anyone else?'"

Many young adults also seem to expect to start out at the level they were accustomed to in their parents' home: new car, luxurious apartment, any electronic gadget they happen to fancy, and money for winter ski weekends. And why not? Their parents sent them to college with microwave ovens, televisions, stereos, Nintendo sets, and computers. Why should they expect less when they graduate? And why should work interfere with what they perceive as "the good life"?

Donna Clark said with a sigh, "I put one precious, bright young woman on a temporary assignment that was the chance of a lifetime. If she worked 520 hours with the company, she would be hired full-time automatically and put on their payroll without paying a fee. She had good chances for advancement, everything laid in front of her. But she moved in with some friends, started staying out late and coming to work late, letting her friends drop by the office as if it was a party. When the company dismissed her, I thought we would have tears. Instead, she shrugged. 'Oh, well, I thought this would happen.' When I told her that those work habits would go on her permanent work record, she looked at me as if I were out of my mind."

Hard work and *responsibility* are old-fashioned words, but like bread and butter, they are important for life. They are not innate in humans, however. They have to be taught carefully.

A WISE PARENT KNOWS:
A child is the only known substance from which a responsible adult can be made.

Thomas Lickona

"When they handle it right," says Robert Barnes, "parents get out of the way and make the child personally responsible, with a consequence if chores are not done. This teaches both responsibility and how to be accountable, which is easily transferable into the adult world."

THE NEED TO CARE FOR THE WORLD

Children not only need to learn to care for themselves, they also need to learn to care for the world around them. Barbara pointed out that responsibility learned in the family has global ramifications: "Homes are a good place to learn to make your environment a better place to be. If we don't learn how to take care of our own little space, we won't be able to take care of bigger spaces. I heard someone say that many of our political problems come because politicians are really children who never learned to pick up after themselves: 'What are you going to do with this nuclear waste when you make it?' 'I don't know. Somebody else will come along after me and pick it up.' We need to learn as children to take care of our own mess."

SUMMARY

Having regular chores and working on the family team teaches children to care for personal needs, maintain a home and yard, value the family unit, respect and serve others, accept work as an important part of life, and care for the world. Children who are part of a team also relieve stress on busy parents.

Is all of that important? Certainly!

Will most children joyfully agree? Probably not.

This morning our younger son came prancing into my study. "Mom, how tall are you?"

"Five-two."

"I'm five-one."

"David! You *can't* be five-one! I'm not ready for you to be as tall as I am."

"Sorry, Mom." Smug grin. "Growing up is one of those things you just can't control."

He's right. Growing up is one of those things we can't control. The best we can do as parents is get busy teaching our children what they need to know *whether or not they want to learn it!*

Before we face the hurdle of giving our own children chores, however, let's fortify ourselves with a brief look at "the good old days" of childhood.

CHAPTER TWO

Fate of Our Fathers—and Mothers

ONE SUMMER MORNING my sons and I strolled through Old Sturbridge Village, Massachusetts. Old Sturbridge is a colonial village faithfully recreated and peopled with inhabitants who daily grow food, churn butter, weave clothing, cook meals, and saw wood as our ancestors did. On the village green, visiting children are given toys from the colonial period for an hour's recreation.

In the barnyard we heard, "Feeding chickens and gathering eggs were children's jobs." Beside a washpot, "Stirring the wash was the children's job." At the village well, "Carrying water was the children's job." Inside a home, "Spinning and carding wool were children's jobs."

Do you see a trend here?

WHAT CHILDREN USED TO DO

Childhood used to be "a brief, unimportant prelude to adulthood and the real business of living."[1] For most of human history, it was taken for granted that children would work in the home and family business. Scripture portrays Rebekah drawing water, Miriam tending her baby brother, Samuel apprenticed to the priest, David herding sheep. It suggests that Jesus helped in Joseph's carpenter shop. Four disciples fished with their fathers.

In medieval times, once boys were seven (and likely to survive to adulthood), they were apprenticed to learn a trade or sent to an overlord to learn to manage an estate and wage war. Their sisters, meanwhile, learned to keep house, sew clothing and linens, tally household accounts, preserve fruit, make perfumes, bake and prepare meats, prepare medicines, and bandage wounds.

In colonial days, when 97 percent of the population was rural, adults considered work a blessing given by God to keep people out of trouble. The Protestant ethic stressed the importance and dignity of human labor. Through labor, both Quakers and Puritans believed, we serve God; an industrious child, therefore, was a righteous child. While modern child psychologists rebuke us for teaching children too much too early, Puritan parents expected girls to knit at four, spin flax and comb wool at six, and use the large spinning wheel as soon as they could reach the top from a stool. A short list of tasks children helped with include, "clear land, sow and harvest crops, build barns, dry fish, shoe horses, spin, weave, bake, feed chickens, saw and chop firewood, tend cattle and sheep, gather fruit, hunt, fish, make brooms, and split shoe pegs."[2] (What's a shoe peg?)

Agricultural families and poor families around the world still expect their children to work hard. One reason Third World families have so many children is the same reason our grandparents did— they need many hands to help with the farm or family business. "Remember Me," a short film produced for the International Year of the Child, describes contemporary children under twelve who daily weave rugs, tow barges, carry water, sort garbage, and collect dung or wood for cooking fuel.

Our own standard of living is such that most homes are filled with "labor-saving" devices. We have a hard time remembering a time without dishwashers, washing machines and dryers, freezers, toasters, steam irons, water heaters, and vacuum cleaners. Some of us can't even remember how we survived without microwave ovens.

My day at Old Sturbridge Village, however, made me realize that labor-saving devices have not really replaced much of what women do; they have just eliminated what children used to do! It currently takes an average of 99.6 hours a week to keep a house if we include doing laundry, making beds, cooking, shopping, doing dishes, cleaning, and doing yardwork. The time spent on housework is not substantially less today than it was in 1900.[3] The difference is that tasks once done by children— waxing floors, beating rugs, hanging out laundry, washing dishes—are done by appliances most often used by mothers. Do you suppose those labor-saving devices were invented by adults who resented being asked to work as children?

WHAT HAPPENED TO CHANGE ALL THAT?

Between the colonial period and the present decade looms both a blessing and a horror: the Industrial Revolution. In the mid-eighteenth century, people invented machines that could do in hours what had taken families days to do at home: spin, weave, cut and sew clothing, plow fields, mill grain, make tools.

The blessing was that products were more easily available and money could be earned to buy them. The horror was that crowded, squalid cities sprang up around factories, and women and children were their primary work force.

This dark period of history would change forever how the Western world viewed children and work. Before the Industrial Revolution, children worked only in protected settings, often in fresh air. Those who worked indoors were cared for and taught a valuable trade. "Now they had no such compensating niceties. The

Industrial Revolution demanded great quantities of cheap labor, which women and children alone could supply, and no particular care was taken for their well-being."[4] Six-year-olds smothered in hot chimneys they had been sent to sweep. Nine-year-olds perished from lack of oxygen in mine tunnels. Ten-year-olds worked long hours and were maimed in factory machinery. In 1820, half of U.S. textile workers were children under ten, working twelve hours a day. As recently as the early 1900s orphans were sent to factories at age seven, with virtually no pay.

While orphans and children of the poor were dying from too much work and too little protection, the increasingly prosperous middle class began to employ more servants. Middle- and upper-class children in towns and cities are pictured in literature of the period devoting their days to schoolwork and play.

There were two notable exceptions: children of immigrants worked beside their parents weighing, selling, shelving, pressing, and otherwise contributing to the family's efforts to make a living in the new country; and farm children continued to help their parents, much as they had throughout history.

THE OLDEN DAYS WHEN WE WERE YOUNG

It still startles me to see my childhood in my sons' history books—and not even at the back! But as I reflect on growing up in the forties and fifties, it seems that most American children had some chores to do. We cleaned our rooms, mowed lawns, did dishes, cleaned the family's single bathroom, did a small amount of cooking, and ironed. I remember very well using an electric "ironer" to smooth towels, pillowcases, dish towels, and pajamas. What I don't remember is whether or not I liked doing it. That must not have mattered very much—either to me or my parents.

Dorothy grew up in a large urban family with both parents working outside the home. "Housework was our responsibility, and that's how we saw it. There was no difference between the boys and the girls. Some of my brothers and sisters grumbled at how much work they had to do, but now they call Mama and thank her for how she raised them."

Sandy, on the other hand, remembers, "My brothers never worked inside the house, not even to bring their own dishes from the table to the sink. My sister-in-law is having a hard time now teaching her sons housework because my brother thinks housework is women's work."

Jean Lush, a former schoolteacher, says about the thirties and forties, "You could always tell pupils raised on a farm. They knew how to work hard."[5] As I researched this book, I was surprised to learn how many of the adults I chose to interview because they are raising hardworking children also grew up on farms. Farm children continue to value work, much as farm children did in medieval times.

Marion says that she took work for granted. "Everybody in our family worked."

Ann recalls that she and her brother had to walk the fields and hack out weeds when they were in high school. "It was a big farm, and at the time it felt like an overwhelming task. But I learned to look at a huge job and take it one day at a time. When I faced writing my paper for my doctoral degree, I felt overwhelmed, but working hard as a child built a habit of hard work and taught me to break off a little piece of a job at a time and do it."

SUMMARY

Children working is nothing new. Children *not* working is new—and that change is not necessarily a good one.

"But children are different today!" you may cry.

Oh? Or is it we parents who are different?

Most adults remember having some childhood responsibilities. Many of us had mothers who worked at home full time. Some of us even had paid household help. Yet, in a world where few mothers are at home all the time and even fewer have full-time paid help, we often do not expect or teach our children to work.

Why? Well, let's see. . . .

PART TWO

Why We Don't Make Our Children Work

CHAPTER THREE

Anything You Can Do, I Can Do Better!

ONE AFTERNOON while my son took gymnastics, I watched several mothers attaching crepe-paper streamers to the gym wall. "What's happening?" I asked.

"Our girls' team is having a Valentine's meet this weekend."

"Why aren't they doing the decorating?" I wondered aloud.

"Oh, they're much too busy with practice," said one.

"They'd do a sloppy job," added another.

"Besides," added a third with a giggle, "we enjoy doing it."

That was my first introduction to a now-familiar phenomenon: parents who do things for their school-age children. Little-League parents construct opening-day parade floats while team members play catch. Parents of high-school band members wrap Christmas gifts in a booth at the mall. Parents sell candy or popcorn at work to support school clubs and sports teams.

When asked why we do these things instead of allowing the children to do them, we give all sorts of reasons: it's too dangerous to let kids sell candy door to door; the kids won't do as good a job; the kids are too busy. Yet our children play in the neighborhoods we think are unsafe for them to sell in; most of us did our own service projects in school; and many of us were also busy with after-school activities. Do we do a lot of things for our children simply because we ourselves don't want to grow up?

Maybe so. But let's explore other reasons why some parents do things *for* rather than *with* their children.

THE PERFECT PARENT

The Perfect Parent knows exactly how everything ought to be done. "I like things done just right, which means *my* way."

Jean admits, "I don't have patience to teach children to do a job right, but if I simply ask them to fold clothes, the clothes have creases in the wrong places. That makes more work for me because I have to iron them over. I can't let them go to school looking as if they slept in their clothes! I know it's my hang-up, but I have taken clothes off my sons and ironed them. When I get a little time to work in the yard, I know exactly what I want done and how. If I don't do it in a methodical way, a little bit at a time, I feel overwhelmed. But on the day when I want to clean out one flower bed thoroughly, they want to mow a little, weed a little. It's easier to do it myself than to fight with them."

Marion said, "I went behind my seven children and redid what they had done, or I wouldn't ask them to do things because I could do it better." With the wisdom of hindsight, she adds, "Now that they're grown, I see that wasn't good. I wish I'd made them do more or left some things undone. My insisting on perfection was bad for all of us. I was stretched like worn-out elastic, and they didn't learn."

One season when I was being particularly hard on our younger son, I had a dream. I was walking along a road with a woman named Eliza. Behind us trotted a small lamb carrying a huge, full basket. Suddenly Eliza called, "Stop, mum! The basket has overlaid the lamb!" That was not the first time the Holy Spirit rebuked me in a dream. I now keep those words over my desk. They remind me not to overwhelm young or fragile people with my own hard standards.

A WISE PARENT KNOWS:
Be ever soft and pliable like a reed,
Not hard and unbending like a cedar.

The Talmud

Putting up with less than what we want is hard, however. When our family sat down to a "meal" of boxed macaroni and cheese and a glass of milk, I demanded, "Where's the vegetable?" and Bob added, "Where's the meat?"

Our seven-year-old's lower lip trembled. "I did it all by myself," he reminded us.

So he had. Tomorrow we could eat vegetables and meat. Today the process was more important than the product.

"But my husband won't sit down to an incomplete dinner," one mother objected. "He would throw a fit if I let the children put half a meal on the table. It's no good to say what families 'ought' to do. The reality is, you have to work with your family around the parents' hang-ups."

She's right. We do have to live with who we are. Some people have a high need for order and perfection. That is no excuse not to teach the children. Suggestions in chapter six's "How to Teach Children a Skill," based on the Montessori method for teaching practical life skills, can help teach children to do skills correctly. And while children are at home, a Perfect Parent may need to shift energy from doing other things well in order to concentrate on doing one thing *very* well: training up a child.

That doesn't mean giving up all your standards. The parent who wants perfect meals can let a child help with cooking. Mastering dishes one at a time as part of a meal, a child eventually learns what a complete meal consists of—and is prepared to tackle one.

THE SERVANT

The Servant does all the housework to justify staying at home with the children. "I do all the housework. Why else does a parent stay home? I don't really need my children to help me keep house."

The Servant, a full-time parent and homemaker, may enjoy being at home, making a lovely, peace-filled home, taking small people to libraries, or kissing bumped knees. She feels so guilty, however, about being "just" a homemaker and parent that she works many hours a day holding up the family single-handedly.

The Servant, sadly, has swallowed a common lie of society: "Parents who stay home with children don't really 'do' anything that parents who work full-time don't also do in addition to 'work.'" If society truly valued homes and children, day-care workers and teachers would earn more than automobile mechanics and football players, businesses would be as concerned for employee families as for the corporate bottom line, and government would be funding parenting classes for welfare mothers of preschoolers instead of ordering them to work. Unfortunately, since that's not the case, it's no wonder that many very good parents become Servants. Even while they delight in pushing swings under a clear blue sky and laughing with their children, they fear that staying home with children is self-indulgent or even downright lazy.

Like the rest of society, the Servant fails to value the role of nurturer, and fails to see everything that stay-at-home parents do for the rest of the world. Employed parents ought to regularly send flowers to stay-at-home ones! At school they chaperone field trips, serve as room parents, volunteer in libraries and clinics, and drive children when other parents are at work. In the community they give hours to charity, hospitals, and churches, supervise after-school neighborhood play, and dispense grape juice, wisdom, and smiles to many more children than their own. But a Servant *thinks* all she does is "keep house."

Therefore, when told that by fourteen a child ought to be able to perform all household chores, a Servant creeps into a private worry closet and panics! "If a fourteen-year-old can do everything I can do as well as I do it, how can I justify staying at home?" The Servant's answer? Don't train the fourteen-year-old to do anything!

A Servant's worry and guilt get reinforced by those who imply that parents who stay at home *should* do everything. I recently read: "In conventional families, adolescent children have only slightly more responsibility for household chores when the mother is employed than when she is home all day." Doesn't that imply that a child whose parent is home all day *ought to have fewer chores* than one whose parent is employed? But why? Will those children as adults need fewer housekeeping skills than children of employed parents?

Servants who home school carry a double burden. Like Susannah Wesley, these parents add a fulltime job—teaching—to an already full load of childcare and household responsibilities. Unlike Susannah, however, they seldom have servants to cook, clean, and do laundry. Do they insist that the employed parent and home schooled children take on more housework so they can do their new job well? Not always. "I feel my children see enough of me and of the house," said one, "so when we finish school, I send them outside to play, then I begin to do the housework. But I never get done. By the time I finish supper, get the laundry done and the next day's lessons planned, I am exhausted."

Stay-at-home parents need to remind themselves often that they have chosen to stay home in order to be with and train their children and, in many ways, to nurture the rest of society. When they are tempted to become Servants, however, they also need to remind themselves that training children includes teaching them how to care for future homes and families.

Elva Anson's *How To Get Kids to Help at Home* is aimed at creative stay-at-home parents, for her chore charts and cleaning games take more time than most employed mothers have. Anson asks Servants a piercing question: "Our children need not to need us. Do you need your children to need you?"[1]

THE SAINT

The Saint makes sacrifices. "Childhood is so short, I don't want my children having to spend it all working. Keeping the house going is the least I can do for them. They'll be adults soon enough, with as many pressures as I now have."

The Saint excuses children from all chores in order to follow Paul's admonition in Romans 12:1: "Offer your bodies as living sacrifices." So why do Saints, like Perfect Parents and Good Mothers, often feel tired, crabby, and guilty about not being nicer or doing more? Because Saints forget that the sacrifice is supposed to please God, not our children! God gives us children to train; training involves more than driving a child from one activity to another, providing pleasure, and supervising studies.

"Many parents think that when children have sports practice and music lessons, that's enough. But these pursuits are disciplines of a different kind that have little to do with basic responsibility to the family. Part of what goes on in the home is the development of teamwork. For family life to function, everyone depends on the contribution of everyone else."[2]

As family counselor Robert Barnes said in his interview, a child permitted to concentrate on homework and personal activities without also sharing family maintenance tasks may grow up to be an adult who sees his or her role primarily as a provider or player.

A *true* Saint knows that discipline, responsibility, and accountability are important for children—and provides them.

THE MARTYR

The Martyr refuses to ask for help. "The rest of the family lives in this house. They see everything I do. I keep hoping one night I'll come home and find the laundry has been done or the floor mopped." (Deep sigh.)

It never happens!

Most people don't automatically sense what our needs are. Or if they do sense we need help, they may have a very narrow view of what "help" involves. "My husband will always wash dishes," one woman said. "Even when I can think of five more important things that need to be done at the time, he heads for the sink. I think when he was young, that was mostly what his mother asked him to do." Does that sound familiar?

James 4:2–3 informs us, "You do not have because you do not ask. When you ask, you do not receive, because you ask with wrong motives." That's certainly true in parenting! Martyrs do not get the help they need because they don't ask. Or if they do, they ask in tones that make others feel guilty rather than part of a family team.

THE COMPENSATOR

The Compensator tries to atone for a child's less-than-perfect life. "My poor child, the least I can do for you is free you from household chores."

One woman tried to make up for her children's chronic illness. "I had low expectations from my children because I thought I could compensate in some degree for the shots, food restrictions, blood and urine tests, and emergency rooms that were often part of their childhood. So I taught all day, graded papers in parking lots, did most of the cooking, cleaning, laundry, and dishes, and was exhausted most of the time. I excused my children from helping at home to make up for their living in a less-than-perfect world."[3]

A WISE PARENT KNOWS:
The only effective way
to protect children
is to teach them
to care for themselves.

Linda said, "We had a traumatic divorce. I felt so sorry for my daughter and what she was going through—separation from her dad and her brother, whom she loved very much—that I hated to ask her to work around the house. I felt guilty for making her do chores. I wasn't doing her any favors, though. It's very important for kids in single-parent families to work around the house. It not only gives them a sense of responsibility that they are a part of the family unit but also gives them a sense of security because they are helping to stabilize the situation."

THE SHIELD

The Shield harbors grudges from childhood. "I remember how I resented chores. I don't want my children to feel the same way."

Ann remembers, "Our house had a one-acre lawn that needed to be mowed every week. With a push mower. It took seven hours! When a child was in seventh grade, it was your turn until the next kid came along. I had five years of mowing before my next brother got old enough to mow. It was a horrible burden, and I would *never* expect that from my child!"

"Yet," she adds with a twinkle, "mowing that yard really taught me to be organized. If I wanted to go to a track meet on Saturday, I had to mow at least one hour each weekday afternoon. I think the reason I don't put things off now is because I spent so many years planning my life around that lawn."

A WISE PARENT KNOWS:
We *sometimes mature as we endure.*

In 1 Corinthians 13:11, Paul says, "When I was a child, I . . . reasoned like a child. When I became a man, I put childish ways behind me." Shielding parents still see their own childhood through the eyes of a child: it wasn't fair to make me work so hard. As adults, parents need to put away childish reasoning and look at even their own past with adult eyes. When we see where hard parts of life shaped the good that is now in us, let's not shield our children from those same difficulties.

THE DYNAMO

The Dynamo moves quickly to get everything done. "I've organized my housework so I can do it in a minimum of time. It takes much longer to teach the children to do it than to do it myself. Besides, I don't want my kids to be doing chores when I have time to be with them!"

Dynamos are often driven by fear and guilt. They are not only responsible for a house but also spend many hours a day either at work or volunteer activities and never have enough time for everything that needs to be done. One Dynamo said, "Laundry is an all-day job when you do it for a family of five. It takes one of my two weekend days already. Can you imagine how long it would take to teach the children to do it? So far I haven't had time to add that to my schedule."

A Dynamo will never slow down enough to teach a child to work unless convinced that

- children need to learn to work;
- working together can also provide quality time; and
- teaching children to work is worth the time it takes.

In chapter one I discussed why children need to work. Working together is the only way to convince anyone that chore time can also be quality time. But proving that teaching children to work is worth the time it takes is a matter of simple math. If we only have to do a job once, obviously it's faster just to do the job than to teach a child to do it. But if a family does laundry one day every weekend for a year, that's a major part of *fifty-two days a year*—almost two months! Which is more time efficient: spending two or three days teaching children to do laundry or spending two months doing it yourself?

Time-management principles derived from the workplace teach that thirty minutes of planning in a week can save seven hours. For example, planning a week's menus and making a shopping list saves extra trips to the store; planning to cook a large pot of something can save two or three nights' cooking.

Similarly, taking an hour a month to plan a family's chore schedule can free everyone from doing too much. "Cleaning this house takes me all day," one mother laments. A family of four trained workers can clean an entire house in about two hours! What *could* a Dynamo do with all that free time?

Our family of four cooks six evening meals and does six sets of evening dishes each week: twelve jobs. (We eat out on Sundays.) Each family member gets three jobs and nine chore slots free. I'm free to write this chapter on a Thursday evening because when I left the kitchen Tuesday night after cooking twice and washing dishes once this week, I was done with evening kitchen chores all week!

THE ABDICATOR

The Abdicator has thrown in the towel. "I'm a failure as a parent. I don't do anything consistently, and I'm probably not doing much well. My kids will have to get themselves straightened out when they grow up."

Linda spoke of a time when she was an Abdicator. "Right after the divorce I wasn't consistent. I found it hard to stick by my guns because I was insecure and shaky inside myself. It wasn't until my confidence built up and I felt I could make the right decisions that I began to expect any help at home from my child."

Many Abdicators are immobilized by that cardinal rule laid down in so many parenting books: *be consistent*. They know they are not consistent—not only is their family schedule erratic, but their temperament is too often like the apostle Paul's when he confesses in Romans 7:18: "I have the desire to do what is good, but I cannot carry it out." And so, knowing that they make chore charts but don't help the family live up to them, that they make resolutions to be firm and loving but then get lax or angry, an Abdicator decides, "I'll never be able to teach my children to do housework or anything else. Why try?"

Abdicators need to talk with other parents as well as read books. Then they will learn that no parents outside of books are *really* consistent. The nature of life is that most families eat at irregular hours, go to bed at irregular hours, and every week have to adjust the "permanent" chore schedule to accommodate somebody's special event. Furthermore, no matter how much we may resolve to be consistently firm, calm, and loving, Jesus is the only human who, to this date, has managed consistently to do so.

Abdicators, take heart! Almost every parent I interviewed for this book worries about not being consistent. Barbara, who is not an Abdicator, nevertheless admits, "I think my kids will probably say about me, 'Her only consistency was, she was consistently unpredictable.' People say, 'My mother always—' or 'My dad would never—.' I have that ideal of consistency, but I can't seem to live up to it. Our kids never know when it will mean a lot that the toilet was scrubbed well or when it will be taken for granted. Maybe we have some consistency, but I don't see it."

Abdicators (and all parents) need to hear the comforting words said by the leader of a spiritual-growth seminar: "Don't beat yourself for what you do not do on a regular basis. Set goals, and regularly evaluate what you *have* done. If you wanted to pray daily and you only prayed four times one week, celebrate that you prayed more than you would have if you had not set goals. Then figure out what kept you from succeeding the other days. What could you have done differently?"

Moira adds, "We always have to be loving and consistent. But consistency needs to be elastic and compassionate, not rigid. Kids need to know that." Parents do, too!

THE SLOTH

The Sloth just can't be bothered. "You kids do whatever you want as long as you don't bother me."

A full-blown Abdicator, the Sloth is truly lazy—or paralyzed. Sloths read, watch television, or sleep rather than doing housework, much less teaching children to do it.

Maria Montessori, the great Italian educator, once said, "To teach a child to feed himself, to wash and dress himself, is a much more tedious and difficult work, calling for infinitely greater patience, than feeding, washing, and dressing the child one's self."[4] Any parent knows that. Sloths have decided, however, that teaching is too much trouble.

I almost left Sloths out of the list, for few Sloths will read this book. But some of the rest of us know Sloths and need to pray for them and show concern. Sloths are to be pitied. They need compassionate and maybe even professional help to wake up before their children are grown and gone.

THE PRIVILEGED

The Privileged can't find anything for a child to do. "My biggest problem," Jean told me, "is finding chores to give the children. Since I went back to work, we have a maid who cleans twice a month and changes our beds. We aren't at home much, so things don't really get very dirty between her visits. The kids load the dishwasher, and they could sort and do laundry, but that isn't very much. Still, it's about all any of us does anymore."

As I said earlier, the demise of rugs that need beating, floors that need waxing, chickens that need feeding, and washpots that need stirring eliminated much of the good hard work children used to do. Chapter seven includes a checklist of skills a child may need by adulthood. You may want to use the checklist as a guideline for training. However, Privileged Parents can also be creative.

Thinking over what she had said, Jean mused, "Maybe we could teach our kids some life skills we don't have ourselves. Gardening, for instance. We could make it a family project—go to the library to learn how, plant some stuff, and let the kids help take care of it. Or we could build a low brick wall around the shrubbery for a planter, learn to do car maintenance, things like that. It could be fun for all of us. Otherwise, it's a real burden to think up ways to teach them responsibility."

I think she has a great idea. Once their children have mastered the basic skills—and since the children may *not* be able to afford a paid household helper in adulthood, they do need to learn how to do the basics—families who employ household help and lawn services may want to consider other skills that could be fun to learn together.

SUMMARY

Did you see yourself in any of the mirrors in this chapter? Most of us see ourselves in several, for we give different reasons at different times for not putting our children to work. Furthermore, even when *we* have decided they need to become part of our family housework team, somebody else may get in the way: the child's other parent!

Let's look at why—and how to get beyond that particular barrier.

CHAPTER FOUR

In My Mother's House ...

H OW MUCH do you know?

1. After a small meal or snack, you should always
   a. wash dishes by hand,
   b. soak dishes to put in the dishwasher later,
   c. rinse and put dishes in the dishwasher immediately.

2. You save time if you take dishes out of a dishwasher
   a. when the cycle has run,
   b. as you need them.

3. The correct way to put on a patterned top sheet is
   a. with the pattern up, facing the blankets,
   b. with the pattern down, facing the bottom sheet.

4. A "clean" room
   a. has no clutter in it,
   b. has been vacuumed and dusted, but a little clutter's okay,
   c. has been vacuumed and dusted and has no clutter.

However you answer those questions, your spouse probably answers most of them differently. Only God knows why people whose mothers stack dirty dishes to wash once a day almost always marry people whose mothers wash up as they cook. It's one of the little mysteries that keep marriage spicy!

For spouses to disagree (or even fight!) over the "right" way to do household chores or over who does what is perfectly normal. You disagree because you each learned those things as a child, and you each *know* you are right. Your mother told you so!

I say "mother" because most of us grew up in homes where the mother was largely responsible for cleaning. What we didn't learn from our mother we learned from our dad—things like changing tires, mowing lawns, and what males don't do. Most marriages have four invisible and not always benign spirits hovering just overhead: two ghosts of Mother and two shades of Dad.

One reason we often don't make our children part of the family team is because we *parents* are not in agreement about what "clean" means, what really needs doing, and which family members "ought" to do what. Before we can train our children, then, we parents need to spend some time deciding what habits, standards, and values out of our two very different backgrounds we want to keep, what we want to discard, and what we want to change.

A WISE PARENT KNOWS:
No amount of nagging will raise our children's standards above our own.

HOW CLEAN IS "CLEAN"?

My first inkling that "to clean" might mean different things to different people came my first year of college. Down the hall roomed two women each of whom had each requested on her roommate preference form a "Very Clean" roommate. Both *were* Very Clean.

We who were only Moderately Clean watched in awe as one of these two women got up every morning, stripped her bed, and left the mattress to air. Each night she made it up with clean sheets. Her desk and floor were a litter of books and papers, but she moved the litter daily to sweep, dust, and polish. She kept a basket in one corner filled with unironed laundry because she never wore anything that wasn't clean and freshly ironed.

The other roommate hung her clothes up neatly after each wearing, but wore them several times. She seldom changed her sheets, but she made a tight bed any sergeant would approve. Her desk and dresser were undusted but starkly neat.

"She lives in filth!" the first would moan in our room.

"She lives in a mess!" the second protested. "She never picks up anything!"

Both of these women were compulsively clean. But who was right?

Our answer reveals more about our own training and personal preferences than it does about the moral fabric of the universe. God didn't hand down with the Ten Commandments a third tablet titled, "The Right Way to Clean." Yet marriages stumble and even founder on the conviction that the way I do things has a divine stamp of approval.

"Household neatness is an emotionally loaded topic, which often has more to do with our own background . . . than it does with children," declare the authors of No-Fault Parenting. "Becoming aware of the motivations behind our standards of neatness can help us to evaluate our expectations more realistically."[1]

Barbara said, "One of the things that didn't dawn on me until we'd been married eight years was that some of our frustrations were caused by the fact that my husband's mom had a house-keeper and mine didn't. That gave us definitely different standards. My husband thought the house should always be neat. He would say, 'My mother was always home for us kids. She baked us cookies and still kept everything tidy.' I know now that most of what he thought his mother did was actually done by the housekeeper.

Since we can't afford paid household help, he's had to lower some of his standards and share the housework."

WHO DOES WHAT IN A "REAL" FAMILY?

Barbara continued, "On the other hand, my father did all our gardening and yard work, and I expected my husband to do the same. He's not the least bit interested. I used to complain, 'This is not really my job.' I've had to learn that in *our* family, it is."

Like Barbara, most of us got our idea of male and female role models from our childhood home. Because my father always cooked breakfast while my mother, a teacher, got the rest of us ready for school, I was astonished when I discovered that other children's *mothers* cooked breakfast. Worse, I married a man whose mother cooked breakfast, so each of us thought the other *ought* to do it!

The question of what is "men's work" and "women's work" has changed drastically since today's parents were children. Today, many—if not most—modern couples share household responsibilities. Judy grew up in a home where the boys worked outside and the girls inside. In her own home, however, both her husband and her sons do housework. "It makes them more responsible. It also gives me more free time. For years I did the housework by myself. I felt it was my job. I worked all week as a librarian, then found myself on Saturdays doing chores while everybody else was out having fun. It wasn't fair! Now when I'm relaxing by the fire, I tease them: 'We all share jobs. Daddy chops the firewood, you carry it in, and I burn it!'"

"Men don't do housework!" one man told me. "Men go to work and women care for the home. That's what God created us to do!"

Scripture doesn't say so.

God had created them partners, told both of them to "Be fruitful and increase in number; fill the earth and subdue it" (Gen. 1:28). The filling would inevitably produce babies, diapers, and child-rearing issues; the subduing would inevitably involve politics and business. Both people were told to do both!

Only once did God assign separate roles to men and women—in Genesis 3:16–19, when he was listing consequences of sin. Man was told he would work hard and sometimes fruitlessly, while woman was told she would bear children in greater pain and yearn for her husband, who would lord it over her. Those separate roles were the first wages of sin. They were also deadly (see Rom. 6:23). Men's primary causes of death are still stress and work-related, while until very recently, women's was childbearing.

Some Christians believe that those who live in Christ's new creation are free from all curses of sin, including the curse of separate sex roles; that Paul really meant it when he said that for those who live in the kingdom of God, "there is neither male nor female, you are all one in Christ Jesus" (Gal. 3:28).

Others think men and women must live under the curse of Genesis 3 until Jesus comes again. Whichever you believe, note that *nobody* got stuck with housework. Men got the world; women got husbands and children. Adding housework to the women's list was a later human development. Sorry fellows, but no man or boy violates God's order by cooking, sweeping, or doing laundry!

Even if we understand that intellectually, however, working it out in daily life can be hard. Dorothy found it easier to teach her children household chores after her divorce. "Now I'm raising them the way I grew up. When I was married, that was more difficult. I grew up making my bed, doing breakfast dishes before I left for school. My husband was never expected to do anything at home. He didn't know the first thing about budgeting, paying bills, shopping, or keeping a house."

Dianne is still happily married after thirty years, but she grew up in a home where housework was shared, while her husband's mother did all the housework. "I have been the one to adjust. I did the housework even when I was working. Each time I quit a job outside the home, it was because I just had too much to do. Our children are now grown, but it never occurs to him that I might *like* to work or that he ought to help around the house."

Gretchen Hirsch, consultant and author of *Womanhours: A 21-Day Time Management Plan that Works*, admits, "The only marriage with which I'm intimately acquainted (mine) is a very traditional one. Though extraordinarily liberated in many respects, my husband is unreconstructed in his view that men don't do housework. . . . Daily work is definitely 'woman's work.' My particular blessing is that he isn't fussy about *what* woman does the work, so he was agreeable to my hiring some day help who happened to be female."[2]

Divorce, capitulation to Western traditional roles, or hiring household help—are these our only options? They certainly don't always make it easier to train our children. In the last chapter, Jean told of a problem she has in a family with a paid household helper: finding tasks for her children. One divorced mother said, "My greatest problem in raising my children is their father. He expects nothing from our son." And Hirsch warns families still living traditional roles in the contemporary world: "A boy who grows up expecting to be catered to will have trouble relating to women; a girl who learns to wait passively for some guy to take care of everything outside the house will be in for a shock. The institution of marriage is changing, and even the most traditional families need to prepare their children."[3]

What other option is there for couples with different ideas about who does housework and how to do it "right"? We can develop a style that suits our family's needs. I remember a friend telling me that when her children came home and said, "Everybody else does . . ." she would reply, "But this is the way *our* family does it."

HOW TO DEVELOP YOUR FAMILY'S STYLE

Most families develop their own style unconsciously, by a daily process of sanding off rough edges and occasional blinding insights. I will never forget one such insight for us when we realized that since Bob hates dishes left in the dishwasher and I hate clothes left in the dryer, we could avoid a lot of conflict if each simply took out what we hated to see left in. Now nobody nags, and we each get to feel virtuous about sometimes doing something for the other. Why did we fight about that for fifteen years?

If a couple finds great differences about standards or who does what, they may benefit from sitting down to consider a family style both partners can live with. "My partner won't do that!" you may say. Here are a few steps that make it easier. They work not only for couples but also for single parents and their older children.

1. *Make a date to talk.* Pick a time when you are both able to concentrate on this one topic. Flinging this issue into a fight about where to spend Christmas vacation or how you discipline the children is not likely to achieve desired results.

Get away from small children. Take a walk by the lake, retreat into an ice cream parlor, borrow a classroom in your church, go for a drive. Sitting down to talk doesn't have to mean perching rigidly on opposite sides of a formal living room.

2. *State areas of disagreement or indecision and write them down.* Stating areas of disagreement means both of you get to talk; this is not a dump-on-somebody session. If one person is reluctant to talk, the other might begin by saying, "I want to hear what *you* see as problems with the way we currently do things." If the answer is: "You nag me all the time," one reply can be, "I know, and I don't want to do that anymore. That's why I want us to come up with some good alternatives." If the answer is, "I don't have any problems," ask, "May I tell you what I see, and then you tell me if you see that or something else?"

Writing down something makes it more neutral. It also forces us to clarify exactly what we disagree about. Is it dirty dishes left in the sink? Who takes out garbage? Clothes left in the dryer? Who mows the yard? Whether housework belongs to one person or everybody? Whether the children's rooms should be always tidy, sometimes tidy, or left to them? Define it and write it down!

3. *Let each person state his or her own needs within the family.* Talk about needs, not wants. All of us *want* other people to do things

our way. What do you *need* that is different from what you now have?

- To catch your breath after work before starting dinner?
- To feel that the house is not always in chaos?
- To face the neighbors without wondering if they are about to give your family a Worst-Lawn-on-the-Block award?
- Freedom to spend weekends doing something besides yard work?
- A chance to accept employment without having to do all the housework too?
- Someone to get off your back about housework?

Each person may want to go away and consider that question for a while. At first you may think, "I need to feel that this house isn't always a sty!" Then, as you think it over, you see that what you really need is not to be wholly responsible for cleaning it or for public areas to be kept neater or for dishes to be washed as they are used or for people to hang up coats as they take them off, or all of the above. Maybe you just need to be praised for what you do instead of nagged for what you don't do!

Work on lists until each states as clearly as possible exactly what unmet needs each of you has.

Note: Are you uncomfortable with starting a sentence "I need"? It sounds selfish, doesn't it? My husband taught me years ago that in this context, saying "I need" is actually giving a gift to other people: you give them your need so they can, if they choose, do something about it. "Unless I know what you need," he said once in exasperation and love, "how can I give it to you?"

4. *Think about new ways of doing things*. Both individually and as families, we have preferences, schedules, personal rhythms, weaknesses, and strengths—and good and bad baggage from our past. If yours is a Christian family, begin by praying to your heavenly and perfect Parent for guidance in becoming the best family you can be.

Then seek your own best style by looking at issues of discord. It may help to ask

- How were these issues handled in each of our childhood homes?
- What do *we* think were the strengths and weaknesses of handling them that way?
- How have others dealt with these issues? Have they found solutions that might work for us?

5. *Force yourselves to name together five solutions.* The purpose of naming five is to make yourselves really think about possibilities, not jump at the first idea you get. For instance, if one problem you have is too much clutter, you might list: (1) everybody picks up personal items daily, (2) each family member picks up in one room daily, (3) each family member gets "demerits" for items left out by bedtime, (4) limit what can be brought into certain rooms, (5) parents collect clutter each day and children (or spouse) must perform chores to earn it back. You might even add: create better storage places and reduce possessions! Talk over which one or two you think is most likely to work in your family, and try it for a week or two.

6. *Evaluate.* After a week or two of working together on establishing a plan and a style, evaluate how the new plan is working. Keep at it until you get something you both can live with.

CHOOSE A STYLE THAT WORKS FOR YOU

No one way is "right" for each family. God didn't create us with a "family cookie cutter." Consider these three ways of developing a family style out of your backgrounds and present needs.

1. *An incorporated style.* An incorporated style selects what a couple together decides are the best of both childhood styles. Carol reports, "We fold clothes like his family did, rinse dishes like my family did, and generally wash dishes once a day, which is different from either."

2. *A new, mutual style.* The new, mutual style fits a couple's own lifestyle and circumstances, and it may be very different from what either spouse grew up with. For instance, when I interviewed people, I learned that many people who grew up cleaning weekly now clean "only when it needs it" or when guests are coming. Donna reports, "Over the years, we found things we each liked to do and things we didn't like to do. By now I do most of the cooking, and my husband buys probably seventy-five percent of the food. As a midwife I have to work so many nights and weekends that for a time we had a girl from Sweden living with us to help us with childcare. We had a hard time deciding to hire her because no one we knew grew up with nannies, but once we decided to hire her, she was a tremendous help."

3. *An accepting style.* The accepting style decides that different styles have equal validity. Some couples decide that each will do dishes, clean, or cook as he or she likes, without complaint from the other. Children grow up trained to do things two ways. "When I clean, cook, or work in the yard, I want to get it done," Jean reports, "so that's how I teach the kids to do it. My husband likes to clown as he works. When he and our son tidied the den one day, I went in and found one with a tennis racket and one with a broom, picking and singing country music. His way takes longer, but they have more fun."

Accepting differences and living with them can be deadly if it's merely a clenched-teeth toleration of another's way of doing things. At its best, however, this style illustrates 1 Corinthians 12: it sees different styles as gifts to the whole family. It can't hurt children to grow up knowing there is more than one acceptable way to care for homes. It may even teach them to think for themselves!

SUMMARY

Scripture tells us that in marriage we are to leave our parents and cleave to our spouse. Do you know what "to cleave" means? It means "to stick to," but it also means "to separate away," like a cleaver cuts meat. If a marriage is to be real, partners have to separate themselves from their parents *and their parents' homes* and stick to one another, establishing their own unique family.

Your family is *your* family. It doesn't have to look like your childhood family, your spouse's childhood family, or anybody else's family. Don't be misled into thinking there is only one "right" way to raise children, manage a home, or function as a family—not even the way you yourself were raised.

And if, even after you decide how to manage your own home, you are still intimidated by your mother-in-law's immaculate house, remember

> *One reason her house is so clean*
> *is that her child's socks*
> *are now under your dresser.*

PART THREE

How to Get Children to Work

CHAPTER FIVE

Start with a Family Meeting

THE BEST WAY to start a family doing regular chores together is the family meeting. A family meeting can be formal or informal, can be held around the table after a meal or during another agreed-upon time. It's essential that *all* family members be present, except, of course, very young children. At a family meeting, the family can set fair rules and consequences, share concerns, settle disputes, make plans for family outings and vacations, even play a game and share a special snack together.

One woman whose family held a weekly meeting when her three children were growing up said, "We reviewed the week and celebrated anything good that had happened, coordinated our fun and recreation times, aired gripes, made contracts with one another for change, and closed with prayer. We decided on chores in those meetings, made sure we played together, and heard one another. Our family meetings were very important for all of us."

"But we can't hold weekly meetings!" you may exclaim in horror. "One parent travels, the kids are involved in sports and music lessons, we have church meetings three nights a week—how do you expect us to get together weekly?"

I don't. Get together however often your family needs it to keep in touch and plan housekeeping routines. Some families find that a weekly meeting is a blessing to the whole family. Others meet monthly or quarterly. If you don't meet regularly or if you set a regular meeting and have to change the time, don't beat yourself. The important thing is not to develop a rigid schedule for meetings but to develop a family forum in which to discuss housekeeping routines, what you want to do together, how things are working, and what changes might make the family work better.

The family meeting is a *tool* to improve your family, not another burden to add to it!

HOW TO HOLD A FAMILY MEETING

If your family has never held a meeting, discuss the idea beforehand. Explain that this is a time for each family member to share ideas about the family. Ask for suggestions for a good time to meet, decide how long the first meeting will be, and set a date and time.

Before the first meeting, parents may ask children to read Joy Berry's *Every Kid's Guide to Family Rules and Responsibilities.*[1] It explains what family meetings are for and contains suggestions for family rules and reasons to have them.

The first meeting will probably seem awkward. Popcorn and lemonade are great additions—they keep it from feeling like a parents-have-gripes-to-air session. Because you may have a hard time getting started, one parent should come prepared with a brief (*very* brief!) statement about what the meeting is about: "We want to talk together about how to help our family work together," or "We want to share ideas for making this a better family."

Someone needs to begin and end the meeting on time and make sure all agenda items are discussed and decided on. Some families feel that the father ought to lead. Others alternate the parental leadership. Still others let all family members take a turn, giving children a chance to develop leadership skills in a non-threatening environment—although younger family members may

---

Guidelines for a Family Meeting

1. Keep distractions to a minimum. Turn off the television and telephone and put infants and toddlers to bed.

2. Decide at the beginning how long the business part of the meeting will be. Half an hour? An hour?

3. Make up an agenda. Ask: "What do we need to talk about?" Rate items A (very important or urgent), B (less important, less urgent), and C (unimportant, not urgent). Take care of A items first.

4. Listen to everyone. Be sure that each person participates without being belittled or ignored and that everyone takes turns talking and listening. Give family members time to initiate ideas, actions, and solutions. Parents need to remember to listen, listen, listen, and be thick-skinned when listening to complaints!

5. Set goals for the coming week, both for individuals and for the family. Put them in writing and post them in a prominent place.

6. Set a time for the next meeting, and put it in everyone's calendars.

7. End on time, even if you must carry over agenda items until the next meeting.

---

question whether having an older sibling lead qualifies as a "non-threatening environment"! Someone should also take notes, and parents will want to approve all decisions.

INTRODUCING THE TOPIC OF HOUSEWORK

Before introducing the subject of shared housework, adults in a two-parent family should have a preliminary conversation to iron out conflicts, as discussed in chapter four, and sketch out a training plan for each child, as discussed in chapter seven. But don't wait to iron out all conflicts and develop complete training plans before you call the first family meeting, or your kids might be grown! At the family meeting itself:

1. *Make a list.* Together list tasks that have to be done for the family to function. Initially parents will need to do most of the listing.

A WISE PARENT KNOWS:
Housework is largely invisible unless it is not done.

2. *Assign tasks.* Decide who will do what for a specified length of time. A child who suddenly feels he or she will be mopping the kitchen forever will be a most unhappy child! Give each person expected to do chores some say in which chores he or she does, and make it clear that initially the family will be trying various ways of assigning and rotating different chores. Stress that this is a beginning only. Chapter seven suggests what chores are appropriate for different ages of children. Chapter eight discusses ways of assigning chores in families with children of several age groups.

EXPECT INITIAL RESISTANCE

You may meet some resistance at first. No, to be honest, you *will* meet with some resistance at first! Three kinds are common:

Resistance 1: "I Can't"

Some people—both spouses and children—when first asked to do housework make a series of personal claims.[2]

Claim: "I don't do it as well as you do. When I do it, it takes longer and doesn't look as good."

Reply soothingly: "Nobody just learning a job does it as well as somebody who has done it for years. Don't worry, you'll get the hang of it soon."

Claim: "I don't know how to do it. Why waste your time teaching me when you can do it faster?"

Reply reasonably: "If this were a job I would have to do only once or twice, that would be true. But doing it every day (or week) means I spend hours a year doing this. It will actually take far less time to teach you than always to do it myself."

Claim: "I have too much else to do." Or: "I *work* all day."

Reply with a smile (after unclenching your teeth): "We all have a lot to do. That's why we need to share the housework." *Alternately,* declare a day or even a week's vacation to demonstrate (by its lack) what you've been doing with *your* time. (Even leave home if you need to!) Or, keep track of your hours and do household tasks only during school or office hours. Whether you are employed or not, what gets left undone will make your point.

Claim: "Okay, I'll do it," (grumble) "but you'll be sorry."

Reply, again, soothingly: "Oh, I'm sure you will do your usual excellent job. And it's not really difficult work. It's just time consuming."

Claim: "Okay, I'll do it, but you are being unpleasant about something trivial."

Reply in an understanding tone: "I know it may seem trivial to you, but it consumes my whole life. I hope you'll agree *that* isn't trivial."

Resistance 2: "It's *Your* Job"

This resistance comes from an ingrained belief that housework is women's work and yardwork is men's work or that housework is grown-up's work.

This belief crops up in places other than families. In 1988, the *Woman's Day Help Book: Complete How-to for the Busy Housekeeper* relegated other family members' involvement to a chapter entitled, "How People Get Help for Free—From Spouses, Children, Etc." Did you notice the word "help"? Before a family will truly share housework, it must get over the notion that some people "do" housework and others "help" and decide that anybody who eats, wears clothes, or tracks in dirt has a responsibility also to cook, do laundry, and clean. Doing housework is not helping one person: it is helping everybody in the family. This underlying misunderstanding needs to be taught experientially and at family meetings.

Resistance 3: "It's My House"

One reason families don't share housework is that mothers—and some fathers—won't really let them! "Women have been labeled as notoriously poor delegators in the home. Many have believed that they could and should do it alone. . . . They have to do everything themselves to be sure it's done right."[3]

Do you know older women who become unglued when their husbands retire and are home all day? Do you know parents who hate school vacations because the children mess up the house? Do you know single parents who complain about having their children for the summer? If you ever hear yourself saying, "*My* carpet needs cleaning," "*My* new chair arrived yesterday," "*My* china came from my husband's grandmother," beware! To refer to or consider a house "mine" is hardly likely to convince others to share in its care. To insist that "my" house be cleaned to "my" specifications will almost certainly ensure that "I" will get to do it!

Letting go can be very hard, but unless we do, we can't expect our family to participate meaningfully in housework. They will be functioning as our servants, not family team members.

DEFUSING GENERAL RESISTANCE

To meet resistance head on, you may tell your children how you feel about having to do all the work: overwhelmed, crabby, guilty about not getting everything done, angry, or whatever your feelings are. Children can even identify if parents say, "It's not fair. . . ," since children use that argument all the time themselves!

Point out advantages of sharing responsibilities—more family play time, less nagging around the house, a less harried parent—ignoring an astute ten-year-old who responds, "What about more harried kids?"

Family members who are expected to maintain a home will probably want to help set family maintenance standards: Do we make beds daily, weekly, or only when we change them? Do we wash dishes after every meal or do we soak them and do them once a day? It's important to make these decisions together; one reward for doing a job as part of a team ought to be some voice in team policy. Again, if this is hard on us, we need to bite our tongues. A parent who insists on imposing standards on a family will probably wind up doing most of the work alone. Worse, that parent is not likely to raise independent, skilled children who can think and solve problems, for they will have been given little incentive or encouragement to do so.

A WISE PARENT KNOWS:
A *child must be helped to independence through his or her environment.*

Maria Montessori

Some things, of course, we will need to insist on, such as safety rules for using a charcoal grill. But families function with all sorts of standards based on the family schedule, needs, and preferences. One author's family has taken the easy approach: "Let's all pitch in, do the essentials, and leave the rest to wrinkle, mold, or wither, as the case may be."[4]

THE BUCK STOPS—WHERE?

Even when the family sets standards for cleanliness, guess who probably will have to enforce them? Mother!

Letty Cottin Pogrebin writes, "I knew a man who never claimed to be too important for housework. Not once in sixteen years did he say that a job was inappropriate for a man. . . . But he also never, not once, remembered without being told . . . to stop for toothpaste or eggs even if he used the last one himself. You know the buck stops with you when the toothpaste or eggs are on your mind and not your mate's, even though you didn't use the last one."[5]

Jean voiced the same frustration. "I still resent being the one who has to do all the remembering. I constantly have a list running in my head of 'What has to be done by when to have a functioning family.' Other family members don't seem to have that same list. They wait to be reminded. But when I remind them, I feel like such a nag."

A WISE PARENT KNOWS:
Nagging is reminding people
to do what they did not do
when you told them the first time.

It's possible, I suppose, for a family to get so democratic and responsible that remembering is shared equally. Until then, Pogrebin muses: "I think, although I have never been successful at it myself, that the only solution is to count *remembering* as labor, and to trade it for other work in and around the house."[6]

It's worth a try. Next week, count "remembering" as one of Mother's chores and give her one less of the others. After all, she probably will do it anyway—she might as well get credit!

SUMMARY

The family that meets together and plans together is more likely to be a family that works together because members are more likely to see all that needs to be done and the fairness of sharing the labor.

But let's change our language a bit now and discuss "learning skills" instead of "doing chores." It may amount to the same thing, but it sounds a whole lot better.

CHAPTER SIX

Teach Skills, Not Chores

O N E M O R N I N G when our younger son was two, he sat at the table and rubbed his nose vigorously. "My nocktril itches," he told his six-year-old brother.

"It's not nocktril, David," Barnabas told him. "It's *nostril*."

David looked at him sternly. "I has to say nocktril, Ba-bas. I's too little to say *nostril*."

Children love to get bigger, but many times they are quite content to be "too little." The same preschooler who will astonish you by putting a tape into a complicated VCR and pushing all the right buttons to start the movie will deny that she is big enough to make her own bed. The child who comes home boasting that he made soup in preschool will insist he's too little to carry his dishes from the table after dinner.

Sometimes we parents even think our children are too little. We still see them as toddlers, failing to notice the progress they're making toward maturity. Every preschool teacher can tell of children who go home Friday knowing how to tie shoes, put on coats, and button them, but have to be taught again on Monday because parents did everything for them over the weekend.

Nearly a hundred years ago, Maria Montessori, an Italian doctor, discovered that children labeled "deficient" could learn more practical life skills than anyone ever expected *if* they were taught each skill step by step and helped to master each step in sequence. Later she tried her methods on normal children and developed an effective educational system that creatively teaches both academic subjects and practical life skills.

Today Montessori schools around the world teach preschoolers skills not only to prepare them for academic subjects but also to do ordinary life activities such as how to cut safely with a sharp knife, how to pour liquids, how to use a can opener, how to wipe tables, how to dust, sweep, iron, fold laundry, and mix orange juice.

"The problem with adapting Montessori methods for home use," says Anne Brandon, director of the Montessori Academy of Mobile, "is that our methods are time intensive. We spend a good deal of time with each child to make certain a skill is learned."

Reading Montessori materials, I found that Montessori teachers do initially spend more time teaching skills than most parents will—especially parents with limited time. What they teach in a few concentrated lessons parents may teach in many shorter ones. But the Montessori method offers wisdom to help us teach our children, whether they are small or nearly grown. You will find, therefore, that the next two chapters are salted with ideas and quotations from Maria Montessori and contemporary Montessori educators.

HAVE A PLAN BEFORE YOU START

Before we look at specific tasks children can do at various ages, we need to develop a list of what practical life skills we want our children to learn by the time they are adults. Consider the basic list that follows. What would you need to add to make it relevant to your own life? Maybe shoveling snow in the North, fighting mildew and roaches in the South, or polishing silver if you're fortunate enough to have any. Keep the list where you can refer to it often, and remember, this list is designed for both boys and girls.

Personal Skills a Child Needs to Learn

Personal care
brush/floss teeth
shampoo and style hair
clean and cut nails
bathe
make dental, doctor appointments

Clothing maintenance
sort, wash, fold laundry
iron
shop wisely
mend rips and tears
sew on buttons, polish shoes
hem pants and skirts

Food preparation
plan balanced meals
shop wisely
cook and bake
follow recipes
set attractive table
wash dishes
store food properly

Lawn maintenance
mow, edge
rake
prune
plant, weed
sweep, blow walks
water lawn and flower beds

House maintenance
strip and change beds
dust, vacuum
clean mirrors and glass
sweep, mop floors
wash windows
wash woodwork
care for plants
use chemicals safely
clean blinds
clean sinks and toilets
empty trash cans
separate items for recycling

Minor house repairs
hang pictures straight
oil hinges
repair toilet "innards"
paint
use hammer, screwdriver, drill, saw, wrench

Budget management
open an account
budget money
deposit/withdraw savings
write checks
balance checkbook

Car maintenance, minor repairs
change a tire
check/change oil
check/add water

Some people may wonder why personal care items are included on a list. "That's not housework!" Maybe not to adults, but to a small child, remembering to brush teeth regularly is as hard, and as important, as remembering to empty trash cans. "I forgot to do my job," Barnabas said one evening when he was four, crawling out of bed. He came back a few minutes later with a gleaming smile. "There! Smell my breath!"

Obviously, we begin teaching simple levels of each skill, then teach more complicated levels as a child masters former ones.

A WISE PARENT KNOWS:
Teach your child a skill today.
A skill is a gift that lasts forever.

We also need to remember to teach a younger child what we taught an older one. "I had high expectations of my older children," one mother recalls. "They had regular chores from the time they were toddlers. The last child came along when they were in elementary school. The older ones and I continued to do chores, but none of us ever expected much from him; we just let him be the baby. Now he's grown and can't do a thing around the house."

"You don't always end up teaching the same thing to each child," Moira points out. "My older son took the public bus to school, so he had to learn that skill. His brother never did that, but because of my divorce, he's been more of a latchkey child. That has given him rights and responsibilities his older brother never had. Recently we built a new house. At sixteen, my younger son was the one who answered questions and dealt with contractors before I got home. I was proud of his maturity."

TIPS FOR TEACHING PRACTICAL LIFE SKILLS

1. *Have materials in an appropriate size and easy to reach.* For young children, teaching skills is easier if "everything the child must use in taking care of himself [is] in proportion to his size and ability;

the hook to hang his clothes on; the places where he washes and brushes his teeth, where he hangs his towel, where he throws soiled clothes. . . . His clothes particularly should be chosen for the ease with which he will be able to get in and out of them on his own."[1] Tiny children need small sponges, small cleaning rags, small buckets, small brooms and mops, small containers of glass cleaner. They need dishes, flatware, and napkins where they can reach them, and they will need a stool for helping wash dishes and dust. Be sure a child knows where all the needed cleaning tools are kept.

2. *Teach a skill by demonstrating it.* A mystery of the universe is how a child can learn to operate a computer merely by being in the room while we do it but can't learn to sweep the same way. As parents, we often tell our children, "Make your bed," or "Set the table," then get frustrated when the child does a sloppy job. Yet most of us would never hand them the car keys and tell them, "Run to the store" when they have never driven before. Doing housework is simpler than driving, but it's just as much a learned skill.

Parents I interviewed stressed the need to teach chores. "You have to make sure they know how to do something before you leave them with it," Carol says, "then training continues when you notice that the backs of plates are greasy, or that there are crusty things along the edge of a floor."

A WISE PARENT KNOWS:
We remember ten percent
of what we hear,
fifty percent of what we see,
and ninety percent of what we do.

Since children, especially, learn from watching rather than hearing, words may distract small children. That is why Montessori teachers painstakingly *show* every step of a process, then let the

How to Teach Children a Skill[2]

1. Be familiar with the skill you are going to teach.

2. Develop a logical way to present it.

3. Take the children with you to get materials so they will be able to find them alone later.

4. Name what you are going to teach.

5. Give the children your full attention.

6. Present the lesson carefully and precisely.

7. Use no more language than is necessary.

8. In general, move from left to right.

9. Let the children join in the task as soon as they are ready.

10. If children make a mistake, don't draw attention to it.

11. Stay with the children until you are sure they can work alone.

12. Allow the children to work as long as they wish at this new skill.

children show the teacher that they have learned the lesson. In teaching "how to carry a pitcher," for example, a teacher shows where to put each hand, how to lift the pitcher, how to hold it steady while carrying, and how to set it down.

3. *Work alongside a child the first few times.* Most of us have gone to a new work situation and been grateful for someone who walked us through our job for a day or two until we got our bearings. Children learning to do chores need that same security. When they first begin to make a bed, it helps to have someone on the other side. When they first set a table, it's more fun if a parent puts out the plates while the child carefully positions each knife and spoon. As children begin to cook, it helps if we cut the tomatoes while they chop carrots for the salad.

This is not, however, the same as having a child "help" you do "your" work.

A WISE PARENT KNOWS:
We are coaches, not slave drivers.

"I didn't learn to cook until I was married," my mother told me. "When I worked with my mother in the kitchen, she'd say, 'Hand me a spoon.' 'Hand me a bowl.' 'Hand me a pot.' I never actually got to do any cooking. I was just there to save her steps."

Teaching a child to clean a room or cook a meal involves a gradual letting go. At first the child assists us. Eventually we assist the child, asking "What do you want me to do?" so the child must decide what needs to be done. In 401 *Ways to Get Your Kid to Work at Home*, the authors recommend watching a child do a job alone three times before turning it completely over. That gives us time to give praise, encouragement, and gentle suggestions.

"While we were learning the principles of work, we also learned there's a best way to do it," Jean Lush remembers from her Australian childhood. "If Father needed to correct us, he'd say, 'Hmmm, let me see the way you're holding that hoe. You know, I've got a really tricky way to hold it. If you shift your hand this way, it's easier.' We watched Father lift his hoe just so, and we'd tilt it the same way."[3]

4. *Advance from the simple to the difficult.* A child faced with the order, "Clean up this room!" must feel as we would if we were told, "Clean up this city!" To begin, a child works better if large chores are broken down into small steps: "Pick up your blocks. . . . Now pick up the stuffed animals."

After a child has mastered parts of cleaning a room, you will be able to say, "Please clean this room." It helps to give the child a complete list of every single thing we want done: polish glass table tops, dust shelves, vacuum rug, wipe off figurines, straighten magazines. Eventually we can say, "Go clean the living room," and the child will know specifically what that entails.

Montessori discovered that some skills are learned better by a process of refinement. Before teaching children to pour liquids, Montessori teachers have children pour beans and then rice. They teach them to spoon large beans before spooning sugar, to grate Ivory soap before grating cheese, to cut a soft food like a hot dog with a table knife before cutting carrots with a sharp knife.

5. *Teach safety as you teach responsibility.* I include this because I failed to do it—almost fatally. Our younger son had been cleaning toilets for several years when he and a friend decided to make a "super new cleaning potion" and started mixing up all the cleaners they could find. Fortunately, the other boy's father found them just as they were about to pour chlorine bleach into the other chemicals. They might have created the best cleaning potion ever but might not have lived to use it, because chlorine bleach combined with acids like toilet bowl cleaners or ammonia makes a toxic gas.

6. *Never redo a job a child has done.* If a child is developing a habit of skimping on chores, we may have to ask the child to redo the job. But when a child has really tried and still has not achieved *our* brand of perfection, we need to learn to live with that—unless, of course, a perfect house matters more to us than our child. It's important to set *family* standards for "clean" before you ask your child to tackle chores.

Make allowances for mistakes. I remember a day when I surprised my mother by cleaning her favorite porcelain figurines with a toothbrush and cleanser. Methodically I removed whatever the artist had put in crevices to give them an antique look. Mother was horrified! But while she let me know I had made a mistake, she never told me what I now know: I ruined them. Instead, she taught me a gentler way to clean porcelain.

Montessori reminds us, "Everyone makes mistakes. This is one of life's realities, and to admit it is already to have taken a great step forward. . . . So it is well to cultivate a friendly feeling toward error, to treat it as a companion inseparable from our lives, as something having a purpose, which it truly has."[4]

A WISE PARENT KNOWS:
Stumbling is just going forward a little faster.

Elva Anson points out, "Many children are taught to be ashamed of mistakes ... [but] mistakes are wonderful learning opportunities.... We need to welcome mistakes—not avoid them.... The important thing is not to identify ourself [or our child!] as a failure. Making a mistake is not the same as failing. Thomas Edison knew that each time he discovered something that did not work, he was closer to discovering what did work. He failed two thousand times before he finally invented the light bulb."[5]

SUMMARY

Something Maria Montessori said about teachers applies to parents too: "[You are] responsible for the atmosphere, the ... condition of materials, and the programming of activities, challenges, and changes of pace to meet each child's individual needs."[6]

That's an enormous job! And since babies don't arrive with instruction manuals, how is a parent to avoid burdening small children with tasks that are too difficult or boring older children with tasks that are too simple? Let's look at what tasks can be expected of children at various age levels.

CHAPTER SEVEN

Tasks for Appropriate Age Levels

A M O T H E R of grown daughters looks back at their childhood: "My girls had juvenile diabetes. By five they were giving their own injections and testing their own urine. The doctors were amazed! Yet after friends came over to play, I always put the toys away because I wanted cars in one bucket, people in another, and blocks in a third. Why didn't it occur to me that a child bright enough to give her own injection was also bright enough to sort cars from blocks? What was really humbling, though, was several years later when two friends came by with children they had just adopted from Asian orphanages. One child was three, the other six. As they played, they automatically sorted the toys into rows of people, cars, and blocks. Those children had learned in understaffed orphanages what I thought my children could not learn at home."

That mother's hindsight gives one measuring stick for parents to decide what practical life skills a child can begin to learn when: consider what a child is doing in other areas of life and match the maturity of assigned household tasks to the level of maturity shown elsewhere.

This chapter suggests age-appropriate tasks gleaned from

Montessori methods, other parents, several other writers, and trial and error at home. You may be surprised to see what your child is capable of doing. As we said in the last chapter, most of us wait longer to teach household skills than we need to. I would warn you from experience, however, that while children of three are *capable* of licking and sticking stamps on envelopes for their busy mothers, they are just as likely to lick the whole roll and create a child-high permanent border for your wall.

PRESCHOOLERS

The question of preschoolers and chores is like Tevye talking with himself in *Fiddler on the Roof*: "on the one hand . . . on the other hand."

On the one hand, some experts recommend giving a child regular responsibilities as early as eighteen months. My own conviction, from raising two children and watching other parents raise theirs, is that starting responsibility that early, like potty training that early, may give you something to boast about but is more trouble than it's worth.

On the other hand, children of two and three love to "help," and Montessori certainly demonstrates that they can, with a good bit of adult involvement, learn to perform many tasks.

On another hand, housework can be taught faster and easier to children who are five and older. Working parents, especially, who don't have time to follow a child around (and others who don't have the inclination) may want to postpone expecting much regular work from children until they reach kindergarten age, when children are in a high-gear learning mode anyway.

On yet another hand, giving a child *no* regular responsibilities for personal care and maintaining his or her own environment before age five results in a child who expects to be waited on.

Parents can either throw up their hands in despair or can look at their own family situations and decide which tasks they want their child to master before age six—remembering that a child needs *some* responsibility at this age.

Tasks for Two- and Three-Year-Olds

load spoons into dishwasher
help feed animals
put away toys after play
wipe table
dry unbreakable dishes
sweep (small broom)
stir orange juice
entertain infant
bring in newspaper
mop small area
pour milk (small pitcher)

dust furniture
dig and pull weeds in garden
fold dishtowels
put away silverware
load washer, unload dryer
wipe mirrors (parent sprays)
assist with stirring in cooking
bring diapers
tidy magazines, sofa pillows
pick up trash in yard
set table (from diagram)

brush toilet (parent puts in bowl cleaner)
take wastebaskets to central place and empty into big bag
pull covers up to neck before getting out of bed
brush teeth, wash face, dress and undress

Additional Tasks for Four- and Five-Year-Olds

put away own clothes
clean mirrors and glass alone
set a complete table
clean bathroom sinks
cut vegetables for salads
help with simple desserts
help load dishwasher
take dirty clothes to hamper
sort clean laundry into fam-
   ily-member piles

hang towels after bath
plant seeds
grate cheese
carry own dishes to sink
mix salads
use scraper to peel carrot
put away groceries
sort wash loads by color
get the mail and put in
   proper place

Before you start pushing your child to learn all the skills by tomorrow, let me remind you that no grades or diplomas are given for doing more earlier. Remember also that a child under age four needs careful teaching, initial help, and close supervision!

Whatever you expect at this age, expect it until it becomes a habit for the child.

Tips to Help Preschoolers Learn Skills

Kitchen:

1. Make a diagram of a place setting and post it near the table for the child to consult when setting the table.
2. Provide a stool, small sponges, and dishcloths.

Bedroom:

1. Let a young child sleep in a sleeping bag over a bottom sheet. It's easier to make—merely pull it up! Or fasten three corners of the bed with large, safety diaper pins by pinning the sheets, blanket, and spread to the edges of the mattress. The child needs to "make" only one corner of the bed because the other three always stay in place.
2. Paste pictures of clothes on the drawers in which they are stored.
3. Give each bedroom its own dirty clothes hamper.
4. Put towel bars low enough for children to reach easily. We put ours on each bedroom door.
5. Provide a big paper bag to store school papers neatly.

Toys:

1. Instead of investing heavily in expensive toys for young children, give them clothespins and a plastic jar, spoons, boxes to open and close or crawl into, tubes from paper towels, aluminum pie plates, and plastic bowls. These help develop motor skills to prepare them for later tasks.

2. To avoid too many toys in the kitchen, store a few "kitchen toys" in a lower cupboard in one large cardboard box so the child can easily pick them up and put them away.

3. To cut down on clutter, rotate toys, putting away half at a time for a month or even six months. Sell or discard broken or unused toys.

4. For easier cleanups, use several small bins for toys rather than one jumbled box. Use bins with large openings, like dishpans or cardboard boxes, and paste a picture on each of the kind of toy (balls, blocks, cars, etc.) it holds.

5. Use large zipper-lock plastic bags to store individual wooden puzzles.

6. A small tin trunk still holds our sons' wooden blocks. It's easy to move, easy to fill, and holds a lot of blocks.

7. Use canvas tote bags to store toys, hanging the tote bags on hooks hung low in the child's closet.

8. Try several methods of storing toys and clothes until you find one that suits you and your child.

PETS AND PRESCHOOLERS

When Jean's son was four, he wanted to keep a stray dog he had found. "I told him, 'Dogs are trouble. You have to feed her, water her, take care of her.' He assured me he would do it all. The first morning he came in and got out a can of food. 'Mama, would you help me open this can?' I basically opened it. Then it was, 'Will you hand me down a bowl?' Then, 'I can't get it out of the can, Mama.' I helped him dig it out, and he carried it to the back door. 'Mama, would you open the door? My hands are full.' Halfway to where he was going to put it, he called, 'Mama, it's awfully heavy. Would you help me carry it?' I put it down for the dog to eat and my son looked at me with shining eyes. 'See, Mama? I *told* you I could do it all by myself!' "

Oddly enough, the child really believed he *had* done it all. As parents, we can eventually train a small child to work alone, but in the first stages, we need to give a good bit of assistance!

YOUNG SCHOOL-AGE CHILDREN

The years from age six to age ten is what some writers call "the golden age" for teaching children to participate in household tasks. Starting when your child is six, gradually add chores until a child has mastered these skills.

Some parents add other skills. Moira required her children to write thank-you notes. "I see that as an important discipline." She also asked her children to read a newspaper a day to keep abreast of current events and was delighted when her older son went to college and immediately subscribed to *three* newspapers.

Dorothy said, "I make my children go to church, just as I make them go to school. If they don't go to church, they can't go anywhere else that week. I believe we are responsible to God to develop good habits in our children. When they are grown, they can do what they like. But I hope by then they will like what is right."

Carol says, "We consider practicing an instrument as a job. Practicing is work, is not particularly fun, and is an investment in the whole family's future, so practice is on our daily job list. We also monitor how much time a child needs to spend studying. Children who must study more hours do fewer household tasks during the week."

What might your family add to the "essentials" list for young school-age children?

A WORD FOR PARENTS DOING HOME SCHOOLING

In addition to household tasks included in your own curriculum, consider this: a child can learn fractions, chemistry, and physics principles by cooking; colors by sorting laundry; geometry by calculating the space to be vacuumed; chemistry from using household cleaners safely; simple math by calculating time for washers and dryers. Montessori schools teach concentration, coordination, order, and independence by dusting, sewing, and polishing silver. They help students develop eye-hand coordination and small motor skills by watering plants from a watering can, using a can opener and screwdrivers, spooning, pouring, using clothespins, sponge washing, and grating.

Tasks for Six- to Ten-Year-Olds

vacuum

tidy own room

cook from recipes

rake leaves

sweep indoors and out

run errands

dust and straighten rooms

use washer and dryer

hem skirts, pants

help clean refrigerator

feed a baby

clean out drawers

paint simple things (shelf, fence)

truly care for pets

clean up after cooking

water plants

take garbage to curb

wash dishes

strip and change beds

sort, wash, fold, and put away laundry

iron own clothes

pick fruit

clean a bathroom

scrape and stack dishes

tend a younger child with an adult nearby

Also remember that other children have school work *plus* household responsibilities. Children who are schooled at home should too!

A WISE PARENT KNOWS:
Habits form character.

A WISE PARENT ALSO KNOWS:
Establishing a habit takes longer than learning a skill.

AGE ELEVEN AND OLDER

Erik Erikson feels that childhood ends and youth begins "when one has established a good initial relationship to the world of skills and tools, and with the advent of puberty." Those should occur at about the same time!

Eleven-year-old children can work almost equally with parents in housework, lawn care, meal preparation and cleanup, and laundry. By age fourteen a child should be able to do anything in a home an adult does. The fourteen-year-old will even be glad to tell you better ways of doing it—whether or not you ask!

"I went back to work when my children were thirteen and eleven," Madelle says. "At that point we sat down and said, 'We are a family. Here are the jobs that need doing to keep the family going.' Each of the four of us now have areas we are responsible for: we each have portions of the house to vacuum; the children clean one bath, and the grownups clean one; we clean our own rooms; and we split up the rest. During summer the children mow the lawn and do all the family laundry, alternating weeks. When school starts, they have to do only their own laundry."

Dorothy expects her young teens to keep their rooms neat, clean and mop the bathrooms, do dishes one week at a time, and mop the kitchen when they do dishes. They also do their own laundry and ironing. "I insist that they iron when the clothes are washed—not just when they need something."

This is also the age to begin working on more mature skills: planning a week's menus, shopping for the family's weekly groceries, organizing and supervising housecleaning as well as doing individual chores. One financial planner suggests giving a fourteen-year-old responsibility for keeping family books for several months—writing all checks (which parents then sign) to pay bills, and monitoring family members' spending habits. Why don't we let them train with politicians or bankers, instead? *That* kind of scrutiny would keep adults honest!

COOK WHAT YOU LIKE TO EAT

The summer my cousin was fourteen, he came to our house to attend summer school. We lived five miles from town, so Mama had to think of some way to entertain two non-driving teens: my cousin and the neighbor boy, who practically moved in as well. She hit on the idea of having them bake a banana cake, which they both loved. The first time they made a few mistakes, like putting half an inch of flour into the pan to "flour" it, but by the second cake, they were pros. Those boys baked—and ate—a cake a day that whole summer!

Cooking appeals to many children, both the junior home-makers and the junior chemists among us. A lot of children's cookbooks contain, however, recipes no self-respecting child (or adult) would eat. We have found that our children prefer to cook their favorite foods, which means they are often willing to learn far more complex recipes than we would have chosen for them.

They each started at age seven making their favorites: hot dogs, peanut-butter sandwiches, canned soup, and macaroni and cheese out of the box. Later I got a looseleaf notebook for recipes they requested. They first chose garlic chicken, barbequed chicken, spaghetti, baked ham, lima beans, waffles, sloppy joes, and turnip greens—which entailed learning to use the pressure cooker. Our younger son was nine when he wanted to learn to cook bacon burgers, so I taught him to make bacon in the microwave, and his dad gave him a lesson and several supervised sessions on "How to Light, Watch, and Put Out a Charcoal Grill." By the time Barnabas was fourteen, he had begun to peruse my cookbooks and try new recipes—most recently Swedish meatballs and our family's first venture into shish kebabs.

Each time they want to learn something new, we copy the recipe into their cookbook with suggestions for what goes with it to

Cleaning Tips to Make Life Easier

1. In a room you are straightening, use one paper bag for trash and one for each family member's belongings that must be taken elsewhere.

2. Pick up bigger items first, giving faster visual results.

3. Start at a door and work your way around a room.

4. If beds are made and floors are clean, the room looks clean.

5. Provide a small basket or apron with pockets to carry cleaning supplies from chore to chore.

6. Straightening before cleaning saves cleaning time.

7. You will always clean most in the room you begin in, so begin with the room that needs the most work.

8. Eighty percent of the dirt is in twenty percent of the room (or house). Cleaning that twenty percent yields eighty percent of the benefit. Which twenty percent should you clean today?

9. Listen to your favorite peppy music while you clean.

10. Iron while you watch television.

11. After an unpleasant job, do a pleasant one.

12. Buy and read *Speed Cleaning* by Jeff Campbell and The Clean Team of San Francisco.[1] I bought it to teach my children how to clean. My husband and I wound up learning as much as they did!

make a balanced meal. When a neighbor expressed surprise to find our younger son at ten making garlic chicken, rice and gravy, lima beans, a fruit cup, rolls, and iced tea, he told her with a shrug, "It's what I like to eat."

Madelle's fourteen-year-old also does a good bit of cooking. "We plan together to be sure she has a balanced meal and all ingredients are there, but she usually prefers to work alone. She likes to take a recipe and elaborate on it."

A ROOM OF ONE'S "OWN"

Parents and children probably have more battles over children's room and how they are to be kept than over any other issue.

At this point you probably expect me to tell you how to get your children to keep their rooms clean. Not me! I have no intention of getting caught in the cross fire between parents who expect children to have their rooms almost painfully clean before they get breakfast and parents like Norma, who said about her six children, "I always thought that their rooms were their rooms. I never made an issue of them unless they really got out of hand, then I'd go in and say, 'We need to do a bit of picking up in here.'"

After living with two sons and hearing and reading many opinions from both parents and children about how a child's room should be kept, I have come to a radical conclusion: the issue of a child's room is seldom an issue of cleanliness but one of control.

For children—who, like adults, come in both naturally messy and naturally neat—their rooms are the places where they most vividly express themselves. As adults, they will have other refuges and other outlets for expressing who and what they are, but for now, almost everything they have and are is centered in that one space. It is, in a very real sense, their "castle." So even when they are very responsible about cleaning other parts of the house, they may fight vigorously to defend their castle from assault!

Parents, on the other hand, are dealing with bewilderment. When did this room cease to be part of *our* house? We usually react by bringing from our arsenal one or more weapons we hope will convince our child to care for the room as *we* want it cared for. Here are some of our more familiar weapons—at least they are familiar to me, for at one time or another in the past thirteen years, I'm ashamed to admit, I've tried them all.

Authority: "I make the rules in this house. You will do what I say!" In this style the parent sets the standards for how a child's room will be kept and insists that the child adhere to them— sometimes even when the standards are inconsistent with the way the rest of the house is kept. Standards may be as minimal as "Make your bed every morning" or as extreme as "You can't leave your room until it is spotless." What is constant is that the standards are set by the parent, not the child.

Reward: "If you get your room clean by noon, you can go to the movies." This is merely the pleasant version of Authoriy. Standards for "clean" and time lines are still set by the parent, and a child learns not to clean the room until rewards are offered.

Guilt: "You really need to keep a neater room. What if Grandmother drops by and sees that mess?" May be escalated into. . .

Fear: "How will you ever learn to keep a house unless you can keep a room?" These two cold-war tactics are often followed by Authority: cutting remarks to induce fear or guilt followed by direct attack, "Clean this room right *now*!"

Shame: "You ought to see his [or her] room. We're expecting the health inspector tomorrow." This style is characterized by saying nothing directly to the child about the room, but often saying things to other people in front of the child, hoping (vainly) to stimulate a voluntary cleaning.

Team Spirit: "Hey, we all live in this house, so let's keep it clean. That's the kind of people we are!" This hearty style is perhaps the most likely to succeed in getting a compliant child to voluntarily clean, but some creative little team members will be offended if the "coach" objects to projects neatly sorted into defined areas all over the floor. After all, that's the kind of "people" *they* are!

What do other parents to do? Moira, a physician, has a reasoned approach: "I don't insist on clean, but I do insist on hygienic. No food scraps and peelings. We don't want bugs or health hazards." *That* is a standard almost anyone can live with!

If you are worried, though, that children who don't learn to pick up their own rooms will become sloppy, irresponsible adults, I have good news for you. Many children who grew up keeping their rooms like middens but who were brought up to be a responsible part of a family unit, have grown up into healthy, responsible, mature adults who keep a reasonably clean house. Apparently, growing up in a messy room does *not* automatically insure an irresponsible, immature adult; and growing up in a neat room doesn't make a responsible, mature adult.

Remember what Norma said earlier, about letting the child's room be the child's room? Two of her sons shared a room the whole time they were growing up. One was very tidy, and still is. The other was very messy, and also still is. The elder one laughs, "It was like a line down the middle of the room. My side of the bed was always made, and sometimes he'd have motorcycle parts on his side." I asked the tidy son whether he wishes his mother had forced his brother to clean more or whether he thinks it could have made a difference in his brother's adult life. He considered, then shook his head. "I did at the time, but as an adult I realize that we are just basically different kinds of people. Making him keep his side clean probably wouldn't have changed him, and living with him helped me learn to tolerate people who are different from me."

A WISE PARENT KNOWS:
My child's membership in my family
is more important
than a clean bedroom.

SUMMARY

What household skills a child can learn depends on what other skills a child is learning in the rest of life. The trick for parents is to increase the difficulty of tasks at a pace that is both comfortable and challenging for each child and that takes into account differences in personality and abilities.

All children, however, have one thing in common: they ask the same questions and grumble the same grumbles. Let's look at their complaints and formulate some answers!

CHAPTER EIGHT

Can Cleaning Be Fun?

SOMETIMES when our sons are scrubbing away at the house, one of them calls to the other, "Are you having fun yet?" A sarcastic laugh is the usual response. After all, anybody who has mopped, vacuumed, or cleaned bathrooms knows that housework is not sheer delight.

That's okay. Neither is life. It doesn't hurt anybody—not even children who think learning ought to be entertaining—to do hard work that isn't fun. But here are tactics that can make work times easier and cut down on grumbles.

"WHY DO I HAVE TO DO THIS?"

Sociologists have established a strong relationship between how people value work they do and how well they do it. Parents who want their children to do good work, therefore, need to let children know that the housework they do for the family is important. This can take the form of praise given to the children, praise shared with someone else in the child's hearing, or just an occasional "I don't know how I could get everything done around here without you." *Parents' Magazine* once went so far as to claim: "Young people will enjoy doing chores if you make them feel that their contribution is valued."[1]

Enjoy? Well, maybe. But if not, at least children who know the family needs their work will take working for granted—and be less likely to complain about doing it.

A WISE PARENT KNOWS:
Cleaning house is a habit.
Children who develop the habit
see it as a natural part of life.

"I'VE GOT TO DO WHAT?"

Children may, however, grumble about specific chores we've assigned. How do we beat that? Give them a choice! Children who choose their jobs have a stake in them.

How *often* you allow choice is a matter for your own family to decide. Carol's family, for instance, believes that a child should keep the same job long enough to develop a sense of pride in it. "About every six months we get out the old chore list and do a new picking round, because some people like a little variety." Other families rotate chores weekly. Within one family, you may even have one child who takes pride in doing the same chore each week and another who takes more pride in meeting a new challenge. One nice thing about parenting is that we are free to try methods, fail, and try another until we find one that works for our family.

The same is true for *how* choices are made. You may try several methods before you find one that works, and even that one may have to be adapted as your children grow older. When Barnabas and David were in elementary school, our family broke tasks into big jobs and little jobs. I put the list of jobs into the computer and ran a weekly printout of what jobs needed to be done that week, adding special jobs like bleaching the lawn furniture or getting the guest room ready for visitors. Family members each chose one big and two small jobs.

When our sons mastered the various skills, we sat down casually before each cleaning and we chose what *rooms* we wanted to clean. Last year, since the boys had mastered cleaning skills, we divided the whole house into three "zones" and rotated chores on a weekly basis, with one person having the week off. For summer, the boys suggested that the house be divided into four cleaning zones with each of us permanently responsible for one zone for the whole three months.

However you distribute chores, I can't stress too strongly the importance of choice. Children who aren't given choices about their lives become rebellious, dependent, or immature. Children who do make choices know they have some responsibility for and impact on their environment. They learn that choices have consequences, both bad and good. They learn that choices can change lives and people. Each time a child makes a sensible choice and knows it, that child takes another step toward maturity and independence. I even read once that making choices—whether good ones or bad ones—is a habit. Children who get accustomed to making good choices about small things, like chores, may be setting a precedent for their whole lives.

Toddlers need limited choices: "Do you want to wear your blue or red shirt?" "Do you want to pick up trucks first or your blocks?"

Older children get a little more freedom: "What are you going to wear today?" "Would you rather dust or vacuum?"

Bonnie McCullough recommends offering children a choice from three alternatives, making each sound as attractive as possible, such as, "Would you rather set the table and make it look pretty, weed one small area of the flower bed, or learn to dust with this nice lemon-scented polish?"

But as they mature, children catch on to limitations in their choices. Barbara chuckles. "I always give my children choices about housework. Do you want to scrub the toilet or mop the bathroom? The kids like getting to choose. But when they were eight or nine, they finally thought of the third option: going out to play. I remember the first time I knew my son had caught on. He asked with a grin, 'Mama, what would you like to do—work, read me a book, or go get ice cream?' He'd figured it out!"

That's why, by the time children are in their mid-teens, choices ought to be real and very broad: "How are you going to spend your clothing allowance this fall?" "What do you plan to cook for dinner?" "What are your weekend plans?" By then, the child will have developed the habit of making good choices. If not, as one mother wisely said, "I'd rather have my child make poor choices while she still lives with me than after she leaves home."

"YOU MEAN I HAFTA DO IT NOW?"

How flexible should we be about *when* a job gets done?

Obviously meals must be cooked before everybody is ravenous, and sheets must be put on a bed before bedtime, but how much choice should children have otherwise about when they do daily or weekly chores? I think the most honest answer is, "As much as you can stand."

Some people disagree. They insist that chores should be done daily just before or after supper and on Saturday mornings before other events. Their families must not have piano lessons on Mondays at four-thirty, scouts on Tuesdays at seven, and Saturday church youth events to plan around. They also have at least one adult who highly values a regular, ordered life. If yours is an ordered family, it may work for you.

Some families, however, don't like regular, ordered lives. Those families may slip chores in on evenings when everyone is at home or they may allow each child to do chores around the edges of other activities. They may not even have chores every day because they don't mind a little dirt.

Are those families irresponsible? Will their children grow up to be irresponsible because they haven't vacuumed or emptied wastebaskets every day? At the risk of making a confession, I hope not! I don't think so either—as long as the children learn to function responsibly on their own family team.

Let me say again: people are different, families are different, and family styles are different. When deciding on when family members do chores, try schedules until you find one that works for *your family*.

But what if a child and parent seriously disagree about when to do a chore? Moira said, "One of our places of friction is that my son wants to stack dinner dishes and wash them early the next morning, and I want them washed before bed. He wants his evenings free, while I absolutely hate coming into a kitchen full of dirty dishes in the morning—even if I don't have to wash them."

Usually in a case like that, parents insist on winning. We don't want our children developing habits of procrastination and irresponsibility, and we do want them to learn habits of neatness and meeting deadlines on time. Besides, darn it, we're the grownups and ought to get our way!

If "when" and "how" become a major conflict, however, *listen* to your children's reasons for wanting to do things their own way. They may surprise you with excellent reasons. If they do, I'd suggest letting them try it their way. A child who can give a good reason is a child who is already beginning to think independently.

IT CAME TO PASS . . .

Remember the old man who said his favorite five words in the Bible were, "And it came to pass"? They reassured him that troubles do, indeed, come to pass. Children need to know that chores come to pass too.

A WISE PARENT KNOWS:
Working together is easier than working alone.

Housework is less tedious if everyone is doing it at the same time. Some families set aside Saturday mornings for chores. We often set aside a "cleaning evening." Two hours usually sees us finished. Another family that also cleans on weekday evenings gives the father Saturday afternoon to himself and the mother Sunday afternoon to herself. Children are free of chores all day Saturday. Imagine the luxury of budgeted time every week to do one's own thing!

Big jobs are less tedious if they're broken into smaller pieces. One year we had an enormous amount of yardwork that needed to be done. We tried working on Saturdays, but we hated spending all day Saturday clearing branches, raking leaves, or weeding. Then I insisted that the children join me several afternoons if they had nothing else to do, but those of us who worked resented those that didn't. Finally we decided that every member of the family would work together in the late afternoon for thirty minutes *every day* for two weeks. Knowing we only had to work half an hour made it easy to get started, and in two weeks we had done twenty-eight hours of work!

If you are having trouble with chores dragging on and on, try these strategies:

1. Agree to work for a specified time, set a timer, then *quit*!
2. Throw a "Cleaning Party" when everyone works until the jobs are done, then reward yourselves with an outing or a family snack.
3. Put on a favorite peppy record and agree to work hard until the last song, then take a five-minute break. Anyone who doesn't work during the music gets a penalty that the family decides on before you start to work.
4. Break a big job into shorter segments, and do one segment today (or this week) and another tomorrow (or next week).
5. For jobs that *nobody* in your family wants to do, plan a "Drudgery Day" at the beginning of each season and do those jobs together.

"I CAN'T REMEMBER EVERYTHING"

From time to time anyone might forget to do a chore, but families that regularly forget to do chores need a chore chart. A written chart is better than verbal reminders because part of learning to be responsible is learning to check the chart.

A WISE PARENT KNOWS:
If you have to tell them to do it, they aren't responsible—you are!

The question, then, is not whether to have charts, but what *kind* of charts to have. If you have time to make creative charts, two books that describe and picture a variety are *How to Get Kids to Help at Home*, by Elva Anson, and *401 Ways to Get the Kids to Work at Home*, by Bonnie Runyon McCullough and Susan Walker Monson.

If you don't have the time, the inclination, or the artistic ability to create clever charts, however, don't despair! A chore chart can be as simple as a large index card listing family names and chores. It can be a weekly computer printout listing who is going to do what. It can be names written onto your family calendar. Linda's teenager, who has a number of family responsibilities before her mother gets home from work, makes her own list of "What I Have to Do This Week," which she initials as she completes a task.

For children who can't read, make a chart from pictures cut from magazines: a tube of toothpaste to remind them to brush teeth, a bed to remind them to make the bed. Glue the pictures to a strip of construction paper, attach it to a blank sheet each week, and have the children stick a star next to each completed chore.

"I'D RATHER BE PLAYING"

Most of us would rather play than work. Wise parents are sometimes able to combine the two, as when Jean's husband breaks up work times by using tennis racket and broom "guitars" for impromptu sing-a-longs. Almost any work can be easier if an element of play is introduced. Madelle's daughter discovered for herself that she works better when the soundtrack to *Les Miserables* is blaring. Whatever it takes, try to make work as pleasant as possible. Crack jokes, find things to laugh about. And you might try some of these ideas from time to time:

Cleaning Games for Preschoolers

1. *Colors and Shapes*: "Let's pick up all the red toys. Now let's pick up all the blue ones." "Let's pick up all the squares and rectangles. Now the toys with round parts." "Let's put all the glasses into the dishwasher. Now let's put in all the plates."

2. *Observer Game*: "You put away ten things and let's see if I can remember them in order. Mary put away a ball. Mary put away a ball and a truck. Mary put away a ball, a truck, and a doll."

3. *Dust Muppet or Monster*: Draw a face on a large white sock for a dust mitt that "eats" dust.

4. *Family Army Game*: Put on marching music, line up at attention, then march around the room picking up toys and putting them away in time to the music. When done, report back to the "General" (parent or older child) and salute.

5. *Ant Legion*: Read Proverbs 6:6, talk about how hard ants work, then pronounce everyone an ant. The ants work hard and fast to see how quickly they can clean up a room.

6. *Do It with Me*: "You make one side of the bed, I'll make the other." "You vacuum the room while I dust it." "You clean the mirror while I clean the lavatory." Tell jokes while you work together.

7. *Surprise Me!* Parent leaves the room after asking the child to see how much can get done before the parent returns. Pops right back in. "I was just teasing, but you don't know when I'll be back next time, do you?" Return when you think the job may be done.

8. *"This is the Way We . . ."*: Remember that old song? Sing together as you do the chore. How many times do you have to sing it before the job is done?

9. *Go Shopping*: Fill a wagon, buggy, or box with toys to be put away, pretending you are shopping. "Oh, I think I will buy this bear. What will you buy?"

10. *Beat the Clock*: Agree to work ten minutes, set a timer.

Cleaning Games for Older Children

1. A *Cleaning Party*: Every member of the family works at the same time until all the work is done. Then everybody gets refreshments and either a family game or outing at the end. Margie, who gave me this idea, said, "My mother did this, and now I do it. When we are done, we are *all* done. And we motivate each other. It's a lot of fun if everyone does it together."

2. *Treasure Hunt*: Hand a note: "Make Your Bed." On the pillow is a second note: "Vacuum the living room." Taped to vacuum handle, "Look in refrigerator." Taped to a glass of juice, "Take out the trash." Under the garbage can lid, "You are done for the day. Thanks!"

3. *Chore Bucket*: Write all the jobs on slips of paper and draw them one at a time. Dianne said, "To make this more fun, I also included fun things like 'Run around the block,' 'Go see your friend for an hour before you work,' or 'Go play for an hour.' The kids really liked that. It was fun to draw and see what you were going to get, even if it was 'Sweep the kitchen.' "

4. *Defusing a Fight*: "Since you are fighting, you must wash windows, one on each side, until you are smiling."

5. *Beat the Clock*: "How fast can our family clean this room?" Give an award for finishing in half an hour, a lesser reward for three-quarters of an hour, least reward for an hour. The whole family enters one room, each member takes one job. If someone finishes his or her job, they help another. The point of this game is cooperation toward a goal, not competition. Rewards can be a snack, an outing, or a specified amount of free time before getting back to work.

6. *You Choose the Music:* Parents agree to let the child choose music for the entire family to work by. Do this only if you have strong nerves or short chores!

Encouragement for Teens

Older children and adolescents accustomed to working need fewer games to get their work done, and some games are more trouble to set up than the chores merit. As we said before, however, even for teenagers, working together is easier than working alone.

Jean Lush recalls, "When my children were clearing the table and washing the dishes, I often made sure I had another job to do in the kitchen. As I put things away in the refrigerator, I told stories about my childhood—just as my father had done. They always loved the ones where I was slightly naughty."[2]

Because older children are likely to realize that some jobs are harder, more time-consuming, or just more boring than others, here are some tips to make it easier for teens and their parents to work together:

1. "Organize jobs by a point system or separate them into categories, such as boring jobs, messy jobs, hard jobs. Let the children choose first from each category, then choose the chores you want. For the jobs left over after all preference picks, flip a coin and alternate who does them, or draw a wheel and spin. Permit trade-offs of two easy jobs for one unwanted job."[3]
2. If a child objects to cleaning his or her own room and you want it done, swap that job for one of your own.
3. Put a teen who complains about working in charge of making out chore charts and supervising the rest of you for a week. Sometimes we all need to be the boss.
4. If you like things cleaner than the rest of the family does, instead of complaining about how the others clean, rotate who cleans what for a few weeks. When it's your turn in

each room, clean to your heart's content. (This worked in reverse for one mother whose daughter is tidier than she!)

5. Encourage the family to swap jobs out of love. When we have adult guests, I may ask the children to cook or do dishes so we can talk with our guests, then I excuse the children from work when they have guests—except for guests who are here so often I don't mind asking them to help.

WHEN THINGS DON'T WORK

No matter what system you choose for charting and doing chores, it will break down from time to time. What works in summer may not work when school and activities start. What worked for young children may not work for older children.

If your schedules, charts, or approaches aren't working, practice your family problem-solving skills. Sit down together and ask: Why is our old way of doing things not working? Do you have a better idea for the future?

Teaching children to be part of the family team is like teaching anything else: it takes trial and error. And sometimes a child has a better idea than we do.

Last summer I reached the end of my patience with David's Lego-strewn floor. We'd tried a variety of storage containers and consequences, but nothing worked very well because he claimed he *needed* Legos spread out on the floor so he could "see them." We tried taping off a segment of the floor for his own private Legoland, but pieces kept straying. Finally, tired of stepping on and over it, I issued an ultimatum: either the Lego that wasn't built into something got kept off the floor, or it got put away permanently for my grandchildren.

Stricken, he disappeared for an hour. He returned with a design for a large wooden drawer on wheels, with separate compartments for different Lego pieces and drawer pulls for easy maneuvering. "I need something like this," he told me. "It's close to the ground where I can use it, and rolls under my bed or table when I'm done."

We went immediately for materials. With my supervision, David sawed, hammered, stained, varnished, put on handles and casters. Finally he painted pictures in each section to show which pieces belonged in each compartment.

"Mama," he announced with satisfaction when he was done, "we've made a family heirloom."

So we did.

And most of the time, it works!

SUMMARY

Cleaning may not ever be the family's favorite activity, but playing cleaning games and working together can make it a lot more palatable. Choosing their own chores not only gives children more control but also develops maturity. You would think that's enough to keep the troops willing to work, wouldn't you?

Unfortunately, even the best of parents occasionally wind up with rebellion in the ranks. What do we do then?

CHAPTER NINE

When the Troops Rebel

BARNABAS ONCE COMPLAINED, "I'll bet the Queen of England never made *her* sons do housework."

"Probably not," I told him, "but you are *not* the Prince of Wales."

Children sometimes have to be reminded they live in families that work for a living and keep their own houses. But Christian parents also have to remember that we *are* training sons and daughters of the King of Kings to take their places in his kingdom. Small souls and small characters will have no place there.

C. S. Lewis felt strongly about this responsibility. Let me paraphrase what he said: "The burden of our children's glory should be laid daily on our backs, a load so heavy that only humility can carry it. . . . It is a serious thing to live in a household of possible gods and goddesses, to remember that the dullest and most uninteresting child . . . may one day be a creature which, if you saw it now, you would be strongly tempted to worship, or else a horror and a corruption such as you now meet, if at all, only in a nightmare. All day long we are, in some degree, helping the child to one or other of these destinations. It is in the light of these overwhelming possibilities, it is with the awe and the circumspection proper to them, that we should conduct all our dealings with our children. . . . There are no *ordinary* people."[1]

We need to hold onto that truth with all our sanity. It will be our pole star as we battle stormy seas of rebellion.

You didn't expect rebellion? Dream on! Almost any child is going to rebel at some point about chores. What do we do then?

SURPRISE—WHAT KIDS HATE

First, we confess that some rebellion comes from the way we assign tasks. Hear what a few children said they hate:

"Surprises—being expected to do jobs whenever my folks ask, rather than their sitting down and telling me what I have to do all week. I feel like a servant. 'Honey, will you please take out the garbage?' 'Honey, will you please do dishes tonight?' I dread hearing them say 'honey,' because I know the next three words are going to be 'will you please. . . .'"

"Surprises. Having my mom or dad add to a job after I thought I did it. For instance, they say, 'Wash the dishes.' Then an hour later they come back in and say, 'Why didn't you wipe off the counters and sweep the floor?' They didn't tell me *that* was part of the job."

"Surprises. They tell me that company is coming in two hours so I have to do my chores right away. I wish they'd tell me ahead of time. I have a life to live too."

What do children hate? Parents who are

Dumpers, who give children jobs the parents hate to do, ask children to do unimportant parts of important jobs, or expect children to wait on them. Most parents hear at least once in their lives, "You just had children so you could have servants!" Dumpers may deserve that accusation.

Adders, who fail to explain jobs fully, assuming a child will know all that a job entails. Children *don't* know. It doesn't occur to them that "clean your room" means "dust" as well as "pick up stuff on the floor," or that "mow" also means "sweep clippings off the walk."

Freewheelers, who like to be spontaneous but fail to see that spontaneity can make life unpleasant for others.

Do any of those sound familiar? Dumpers, Adders and Freewheelers get *and deserve* children who rebel. We eliminate a lot of grief by

- giving regular chores instead of occasional requested ones;
- teaching children exactly what each job entails, and
- notifying the family at once about schedule changes.

NOBODY HAS THE TROUBLES I'VE GOT!

If your child never says, "Nobody else has to do this but me," your kids must be the ones our kids talk about all the time: that vast, invisible majority of children who *never* have chores.

Some children *don't* have as many chores as others. We have a young friend who flings himself in front of our refrigerator every time his mother comes to pick him up so she won't see our chore chart. We had another small friend who didn't have to do anything at home—and used to beg to help our sons with their chores!

Divorced families with two custodial parents experience "Nobody else has to do all this!" with a different slant: "I don't have to do all this at my *other* house!"

One divorced mother's greatest problem in getting chores done is the children's father. "When they go to his house, he makes our daughter do everything. He leaves dishes for days for her to wash. But our son is expected to do nothing, so he complains and cries when I ask him to work at my place."

A single father voices a similar frustration: "My child is being raised by someone who picks up after him. He acts like he will have servants all his life. Because I don't have him all the time, I hate to spend our whole time together griping about dirty dishes in the sink or clothes on the floor. What can I do?"

Just saying, "We don't do it that way at *this* house" seldom ends the conversation. Children want to know why our house rules are different, why we think they are better than the less-stringent rules all other children seem to have.

Not too long ago Barnabas was ironing his Sunday clothes—and complaining bitterly. Each wrinkle he ironed out made a new one. Finally he flung at me, "*You* are supposed to do this!"

"No, I'm not," I told him (for the millionth time). "I'm not supposed to wipe your bottom, tie your shoes, brush your hair, or iron your clothes. All of those are things you will have to do as an adult, and you have to learn how."

Sheepishly, he grinned. "Well, it was worth a try."

Children are more likely to hear us if we say, "I [or we] want you to be able to take care of yourself and your family when you grow up. God gave you to me, and I'm doing what I really feel is best for you—teaching you to be responsible and capable." Relating household skills to personal skills they learned long ago *and know they prefer doing for themselves* can help them understand why they are learning new skills now.

That seems finally to be sinking in around our house. When Barnabas heard that a friend's daughter was planning to come home "to get her act together" after college, he asked, curiously, "Why didn't she get it together before she grew up?"

Children don't often think seriously, however, about being grown up. They don't see that they're training to be responsible, capable adults. They only see that they're asked to wash dishes when their favorite show is on television. At these times, "It's not fair!" rings through the house.

"Fair" is possibly the most often used word in children's vocabulary. Adults may have been conditioned by experience to think life isn't always fair, but children know it *ought* to be. A banner on my father's study wall says, "To believe in God is to know all the rules will be fair and there will be wonderful surprises." A child is born believing that life is fair and trusting us to believe it too. And when a child perceives that parents *aren't* fair, battle rages!

A "Fairness" Approach to Family Conflict[2]

- Sit down together and agree to work for a fair solution.
- Let each person state the problem as s/he sees it.
- Have each repeat back what s/he heard the other(s) say.
- List together *all* possible solutions.
- Select together solutions *all* feel are fair.
- Write and sign an agreement about what will happen.
- Set up a date for follow-up discussion and evaluation.

Some family conflicts can be settled quickly by letting each side state what they see as "fair." When we asked, "If we drive you to baseball practice and spend an hour waiting for you, what is *fair* for you to do in exchange?" our boys had several good suggestions. As you talk things out, you may discover that what your children object to is not washing dishes but washing them during their favorite show. If so, they may see altering the dishwashing schedule as a "fair" solution.

YOU HEARD WHAT I SAID!

Sitting down to talk things over solves many problems, but when a child is in a real snit about doing chores, we parents often talk too much. We remind, coax, nag, and sometimes even threaten. Yet repeatedly telling a child to do something and then discussing it ad nauseum is seldom the most effective way to get a job done—especially by teenagers.

A WISE PARENT KNOWS:
*There's nothing wrong with teenagers
that reasoning with them won't aggravate.*

Instead of joining in a tirade, keep a family chore chart or rules-and-consequences sheet on your bulletin board or refrigerator. Walk literate children over to it. They can read for themselves what they are supposed to do and what will happen if they don't.

Humor may also work. One author recommends that when a child is voicing a particularly good complaint, a parent could say, "Slow down. I want to write all those excuses on this paper. We'll number them and next time you can just refer to the number."[3] That may tickle a child's funny bone and defuse a tirade. We need to remember, however, the admonition in Ephesians 6:4, often translated, "Don't provoke your children to anger." If our teasing makes a child angrier, use gentleness. You may also fight a potential tirade by promising to come back when they really want to discuss things and then leaving the room.

I'LL DO IT LATER

"I'm going to clean my room as soon as I finish putting this Lego castle together."

"I'll wash dishes as soon as this program is over."

"I'll start cleaning as soon as Sissy starts."

With all the excuses children have for putting off work, don't you marvel that anything ever gets done?

A WISE PARENT KNOWS:
Procrastination is often silent rebellion.

Children, like adults, may procrastinate because a job looks hard or unpleasant. Children may also procrastinate to get more attention from a parent—even if the attention is negative.

That's why a chore list is good. Instead of reminding a child of forgotten chores, a parent can ask, "What you are supposed to be doing?" "Tell me what you must do before bedtime," or "Have you checked the chore chart?"—then give the child more attention for remembering than for forgetting.

When a child is putting off a job because it looks hard or unpleasant, try these strategies.

Tips to Help Procrastinators

1. Break a big job into small pieces. A child having trouble cleaning a room may be able to list with a parent various pieces of that job—pick up toys, sweep the floor—and choose one to begin with.

2. Make unpleasant chores easier by doing them together or by planning a big reward when they are done.

3. Would it help to have someone nearby? My son doesn't like mowing, but he doesn't complain if I do yardwork at the same time.

If a procrastinator continues to procrastinate, a lot of us have reacted at least once as Dianne did: "One day I really lost it. My kids got sidetracked when they were supposed to be cleaning their rooms. They dawdled, played with toys instead of putting them up. I reminded them three times, but I was too busy doing something else to stay with them. Finally I got so angry that I went in and dumped out every single drawer onto the floor. 'Now clean it!' I ordered. It took them a week, but they did it. After that when I said, 'Move,' they moved. I'm not proud of that day, but my sons still remember it."

I don't think it hurts children to see parents lose their tempers once in a while. Watching us struggle with our own faults is one way to teach them to struggle with theirs. I also know that one big punishment gets better results than a string of small, weak ones. My father chided me for not punishing two-year-old Barnabas when he disobeyed, "If you'd punish him firmly one time, you wouldn't have to do it so often."

But punishment and losing tempers get less effective the more we do it. Therefore, let's consider a more effective way to deal with procrastination, growls, and rebellion: the truth of consequences.

CHAPTER TEN

Teaching by Consequences

LAST WINTER our son David lost his coat. Since he rides a city bus to school and has to wait on a windy corner, the next morning we searched frantically. "Did you leave it at John's?" I demanded. "Could it be in your locker?" Finally, fuming, I went to fetch my car keys.

In shirt sleeves, he shouldered his backpack, picked up his lunch box, and started for the door. "Mama," he said between clenched teeth, "let me do my *own* suffering."

He was wiser—and stronger—than I. I let him go, but the whole time he was shivering at the bus stop, I was holding onto the seat of my chair to keep from going after him in the car. It's *hard* to watch our children suffer when we can do something about it.

Yet children who learn to do their own suffering for their own actions grow up to be responsible adults. Parents who don't let children suffer consequences at age six may be bailing them out of jail when they are sixteen.

Consequences come in at least three types: natural, related, and imposed. Let's consider how to use each as a teaching tool.

NATURAL CONSEQUENCES

Adults experience natural consequences all the time. We go on a spending spree and have no money left for bills. We overeat and gain weight. God gives natural consequences to teach us lessons.

Ever since Eve and Adam ate the forbidden fruit, people have been suffering unpleasant consequences of their actions. As our children experience logical consequences of what they fail to do, they learn to do things well, on time, and with a minimum of complaint. But the hardest part for me is letting my children *suffer* natural consequences.

Some natural consequences happen without our involvement. A child who leaves a bike in the driveway may end up with a crushed bike. A child who leaves a favorite doll out in the rain may end up with a ruined doll. The trick for parents is not to rush out and buy a new one but to sympathize with the child. "I'm so sorry, dear. I know you wish you had brought it in." Then leave the child to his or her grieving—avoiding the almost overpowering temptation to say, "I told you so." If you feel your child simply can't function socially on your block without a replacement doll or bike, at least wait until the next birthday or Christmas to get one. Waiting and watching other children playing with theirs may teach a bigger lesson than any parent could devise.

Other natural consequences have to be decided on: if you leave dishes on the table after a meal, you eat on them for your next meal; if you don't put clothes in the hamper, they don't get washed; if you don't turn dirty clothes right-side out, they get washed and folded the way they are put into the hamper.

A WISE PARENT KNOWS:
All we have to do
to impose natural consequences
is stay out of the way.

Ask yourself this important question: What am I doing for my child that, if left undone, would soon teach the child to care for part of his or her own world?

A few natural consequences may be too great for a child to bear. One eight-year-old left his older brother's expensive bike in the front yard and it got stolen. If his parents had expected him to pay for the entire bike, it would have taken his total earnings for years to come, and he couldn't have bought a bike until his brother was in college. The family decided on a combination of consequences and punishment that the child knew was related to his carelessness. The boy had to turn over half his weekly income to his older brother for several months, *and* he had to see that all the family bikes were in the garage each evening for a year.

RELATED CONSEQUENCES

When our boys were small, we used the potty-train-your-child-in-one-day method. Besides gaining freedom from diapers, I also gained a lesson in how to set and enforce a related consequence. The method was simple: if a child had a potty accident, he had to "practice correct behavior" five times. He was taken to the place where the accident occurred, then made to run quickly to the potty, pull down his pants, sit on the potty, jump up, and return to the scene of the accident for another practice. This method took a lot of time for a few days, but it meant that I didn't get angry and the child practiced the skill to get it right.

This method has many applications. A child who doesn't take dishes to the sink can be made to practice carrying them five times after each "forgetting." A child who doesn't hang up towels can be made to hang them up five times. A child who consistently fails to take out the garbage can practice until he or she gets it right.

Carol uses another approach. "At our house, if your dishes aren't done when they're supposed to be, every dish that accrues after that until it's your turn to do them again belongs to you too. With seven people at home, dishes really pile up. Recently one of our sons failed to do one meal's dishes and had to do five days' dishes in a row. He never let them pile up again! When one of our daughters didn't do them for two days and started whining about how many there were, I heard him tell her, 'That's just the way it is, kid.'"

Other related consequences:

- Refuse to cook unless the kitchen is cleaned up after snacks.
- Charge a nickel for lights, radios, or televisions left on. Use the money to help pay the power bill. Works for water too.
- Unplug appliances left on: leave the appliance unplugged one day for the first infraction, one week for the second.
- Set a day by which the job must be done, and if it's not done by the parents' bedtime, wake the child to do it. "It's still today, you have one hour."

Stumped for a consequence? Ask the children. They are whizzes at deciding what is fair—especially for one another!

IMPOSED CONSEQUENCES

If children refuse to clean their rooms, a natural consequence is that they live in a dirty room. If that is more painful for you than for them, you might set a related consequence: "I will not enter your room to remove or bring laundry until you clean it." An imposed consequence could be, "You will not eat again until this room is clean." This doesn't prevent the child from eating, but it might postpone it a bit.

Almost every parent I interviewed imposes the same consequence for teenagers: "You can't go where you want to go until your work is done." From the number of parents who use it, I assume it works. Other ideas include

- A "Put Away Box" to impound items left lying around. Offenders have to pay a fine or do one small chore to redeem possessions.
- Withhold some of a child's allowance if jobs are not done or not done on time.

- A "Toy Monster." One father painted a bag to look like a monster. Each evening he goes around the house making monster noises and "eating" up toys left out. The toys are spit out each Saturday and may be kept only if they are put away at once.

Imposed consequences may not have the same impact as natural ones, but they do correct behavior—*if* we enforce them.

RULES WORK ONLY IF WE DO

Picture this. You and your children are playing "Go Fish" when a preschool neighbor shows up. He accepts your invitation and plays four or five hands before his mother arrives.

"What are you doing here?" she demands. "Don't you know you're grounded for what you did yesterday? You're not to leave the property for three days!"

"He's been here nearly an hour," you may point out.

"I knew where he was, but I didn't have time to come get him." She turns to the child. "Now come home and get your hands washed. We're going to the movies."

A WISE PARENT KNOWS:
Children do
what is **really** *expected of them.*

Enforcing consequences for breaking rules is hard. It requires sacrifices and consistency on our part. Families with too many rules and imposed consequences, therefore, are likely to have frazzled, sharp-tongued parents and little real discipline. It's good to look at our consequences from time to time and ask ourselves: Can we replace any imposed consequences with natural or related ones? They're so much easier to enforce.

We parents simply *must* enforce the rules we make. Otherwise we teach our children that it's possible to sneak, cheat, or beg out of anything. That's a dangerous lesson.

One morning as I waited in the county health department for a shot, I watched a mother and her toddler. It was obvious that the toddler wanted his mother's keys. At first the mother said no but then jangled the keys out of the toddler's reach. He begged. She refused. He begged again. And again. After the fifth beg, the mother dropped the keys into his hands and grinned at her neighbor. "He likes that game." Will *she* like it when he's seventeen?

After a child is old enough to reason, the most effective rules and consequences are those set by the whole family. Setting family rules and consequences not only yields rules that work but also gives children practice in thinking about the relationship between behavior and results.

While writing this chapter I asked Barnabas, "Do you prefer punishment or a consequence?"

With his usual wisdom, he replied, "They are really the same thing with a different name, but a consequence feels better. Punishment doesn't have anything to do with the crime. A fair consequence is one that fits the crime." At every age, we can count on our children's desire to be treated fairly.

I've noticed that one theory about consequences isn't always true. The theory is this: since both parents and children have agreed on the consequences, they both know the parent is enforcing a consequence, not punishing the child. Therefore the child doesn't get angry with the parent, and the parent—who is not being an ogre—can give the child a big hug after enforcing the consequence, which both will enjoy.

Actually, many times the child *will* feel as if the parent is punishing and will get furious. The parent *will* feel like an ogre. The parent may want to hug and forget, while the child—nursing bruised feelings and esteem—hunches up a shoulder and moves away. The best thing I've found to do in that case is to allow the child space and time to recover, then show up with cookies and milk and talk as if nothing had happened. Children have their pride too.

BE ANGRY BUT DON'T SIN

Sometimes all of our efforts to help our children feel the consequences of their misbehavior fail. What are we to do then? Child psychologists suggest that if children don't do chores well, or on time, it may help to ask them some questions with the goal of helping them own up to their lack of responsibility. In a gentle, respectful voice, ask

"What are you doing [or did you do]?"

"What should you be doing [or have done]?"

"What is our rule about that?"

"What are the consequences?"

That works sometimes. It almost always works for people like my calm, temperate husband, who can look at you and say quietly, "I'm angry with you"—and mean it. If I can look you in the eye and say calmly "I'm angry," I'm not!

So what are parents who get visibly, physically angry supposed to do when we come home exhausted and find that tonight's cook has gotten engrossed in television and failed to start supper? What are we supposed to do on the morning we reach for clean underwear and find that this week's laundry wasn't done? Obviously we can't speak calmly. Not with hot anger boiling inside us like lava in Vesuvius!

A first thing we can do is not feel guilty about feeling angry. God made some of us with hotter tempers than others. He tells us in Ephesians 4:26 that it's okay to get angry, but he warns us not to let anger lead us into sin.

I suggest that parents with tempers prepare for times when our own consequences for a child's failure to do a job are currently greater than the child's. Post those four good questions on the refrigerator (or paint them across the living room wall). Beside the questions, post family rules and consequences. If you are unable to speak without screaming, merely point the child in that direction. Then try to think up a way to minimize your own consequences for *their* failure to perform.

"I just went and got myself a pizza," one mother told me. "I was worn out, I had work I needed to do that evening, and there he sat watching cartoons. So I went and got his favorite kind of pizza—and ate every bite of it myself. Then, when he felt bad and I felt better, I told him that he could have cereal, which he hates, and we would talk about this another time, when I wasn't so mad."

But whether our anger boils out or gets expressed "decently and in order," as my Calvinist friends would say, parents need to take care to avoid sinning against their children in anger. Let's look at some of the ways we do.

Sin 1. *We punish excessively.* Few forgotten chores put human life in jeopardy. They may make the family wait for dinner or embarrass us when Aunt Sadie arrives to find a littered living room, but children commit far more misdemeanors than capital offenses.

A WISE PARENT KNOWS:
Never use a cannon
when a water pistol will do.

When a child's infractions are of the water-pistol variety, bringing out cannons to deal with them doesn't teach the child to do the chore next time; it may only teach the child to be vengeful. When we find ourselves using cannons for water-pistol offenses, we need to remind ourselves of God's character: "The Lord is compassionate and gracious, slow to anger, abounding in love. He will not always accuse, nor will he harbor his anger forever; he does not treat us as our sins deserve or repay us according to our iniquities. For as high as the heavens are above the earth, so great is his love for those who fear him" (Ps. 103:8–11).

Let's not punish our children beyond what their offenses deserve. Long before the Wright brothers invented the airplane, they took apart their mother's sewing machine. She just made them put it back together. What if she had punished them so drastically that they never again experimented with machinery?

Sin 2. We diminish the child instead of rebuking the behavior. One day when Barnabas was three, he and I had had a rough day. "I hate you!" he roared at me.

"Do you really?" I asked, hurt.

He considered. "No. You hate me. You say so all de time."

"I *never* told you I hated you," I insisted.

"You acted like it all day," he retorted.

He was right. I had spent the day not just correcting his behavior but treating him like a small person who didn't deserve to live in my world.

We parents need to listen to our words *and* our tone of voice and beware if we are treating our children like people who *always* do wrong, *never* do right, and for whom there is not a shred of hope for improvement. No matter how often we have to punish a child or enforce a consequence, we need to remind our children that they are deeply loved. And we need to remind ourselves that we live not with perfect children but with children under construction.

Sin 3. We expect all family members to be alike, so we punish children for being different. One morning David couldn't find his homework. "I put it right on that chair!" he raged. "Why isn't it there now?" I gave him yet another lecture about putting things away, not down, and sent a very dejected and furious boy to school.

Later I realized what had happened: Barnabas had used the chair for his morning devotions, laying the papers on the floor beside his own schoolbooks. I'd put them in Barnabas' backpack while he was taking out garbage for me.

I sank into a chair to pray out my frustration. "Why does David expect he can just put things down anywhere and find them there later? Why doesn't he learn to put things away safely?"

In the quiet, I suddenly knew. As the baby in the family, David has never had what the rest of us have: a younger child around. We have to work more with him than we did with Barnabas to put his things away, because Barnabas' little brother had trained him!

One of the hardest parts about parenting is accepting that no two children are alike, and they must be raised differently. Some children, like some adults, are dashers, hurrying through jobs and moving onto something else. Some are dancers, dreaming their way through tasks. Some prefer to work with other people; some prefer to work alone. Some work better in the morning, some better in the evening. Some want to spend Saturdays on chores; others want Saturdays free. Some get instructions by hearing them; others do better with a written list. Some want detailed instructions about how to do a chore; others want the thrill of discovery. Some get right to work; others need a growl before they start. As we set family rules and schedules, therefore, parents need to accept and even to celebrate our children's differences, not treat them as if they are all alike.

Carol, who has five children, said, "Children are very different, so you deal with them differently. Our oldest daughter is very neat and organized, so she likes to do a job at once and in a methodical manner. The middle one is more likely to do first what she *wants* to do, then do her chores if there is time. It would never work to treat them alike."

Marion, who raised seven, said, "In a big family, you see a lot of differences in children. Some volunteer to work more quickly than others. I have some self-starters and others you couldn't start with a jumper cable."

We must know our children and adapt our training, rules, and consequences to fit their uniqueness.

Sin 4. We throw in the towel when they complain. One mother told me why she doesn't make her children do chores. "They were so obnoxious about it, I gave up. It wasn't worth the hassle."

Robert Barnes's book *Who's in Charge Here? Overcoming Power Struggles with Your Kids* offers many good ideas for helping parents deal confidently and lovingly with rebellion. "Responsibility is the key," Barnes declares. "The child must be placed in a position of being responsible for his [or her] behavior. The parent must be in the position of loving the child while upholding the behavioral boundaries."[1]

To reduce conflict and deal with it, Barnes urges parents to create a parenting plan for each child—a plan that includes discipline, instilling responsibility, permitting a child to learn through failure, and moving a child through phases of maturity until he or she is ready for structured freedom in high school. When parents have formulated a plan, Barnes encourages them to state the reason for the new plan to the child, carefully explain the plan, and follow through on consequences. He advises:

> Parents must go to the effort of creating the plan that holds the family together. Homes need a disciplinary plan so that the family members can have fun and enjoy each other's company. Loving the children isn't enough. Parents must like their children enough to want to set the boundaries that the family can play in. As parents, we cannot afford to fail in this. As the old adage says, by failing to plan we will be planning to fail, and the cost of that failure is too great. What we do today might just affect the generations to come.[2]

Is making children do chores worth the hassle? Not if the only result is a clean house. But remember what C. S. Lewis said: We are training eternal beings.

So what if they get obnoxious from time to time—or even most of the time? Take comfort from these words: "Their disapproval is only unpleasant, not life-threatening. . . . Keep your sense of humor; a well-timed laugh can defuse many an explosive situation. Empathize copiously—and don't give an inch!"[3]

SUMMARY

All children rebel from time to time about doing household chores. The most patient parents get frustrated. But allowing our children to feel the consequences of their actions is the most effective way of teaching them responsibility.

But what about rewards? Are they appropriate, or do they merely bribe children to work? Let's think about that.

CHAPTER ELEVEN

Bribing Your Kids to Work

HOUSEWORK is its own reward. It results in a clean, relaxing place to play, read, rest, and entertain. And, of course, growing up mature is the reward a child gets for doing chores.

Sure.

But try convincing your child! When I asked David to suggest a title for this chapter, he immediately came up with the one above. (He also suggested I next write a book titled *Spoil Children Rotten While You Still Have Them Around*.)

He raises a hot issue: What is the best way to reward a child for chores well done? Do praise and money *reward* children, teach them independence and the value of hard work? Or do praise and money *bribe* children, teach them to work only when a bribe is dangled in front of their noses?

TO PRAISE OR NOT TO PRAISE

I was astonished to learn of the considerable debate among childhood educators about whether or not to reward children's work with praise.

Some authors urge parents to use remarks like "How this room sparkles!" and "That kitchen looks like it belongs in a magazine!" Bonnie McCullough lists 129 ways to encourage and praise your children, including "An elegant job!" and "That looks like it's going to be a great job!" Robert Barnes leaves small notes on a door: "I passed your room and it looks great!" One author suggests making rewards stickers: "Best job of cleaning this week!" "Best organized toy cabinet." The child who collects six stickers chooses a video for the family to watch.

On the other side of this debate stand people who have spent years watching the results of praising children. They have discovered that "once children receive external rewards such as praise, they often focus more on them rather than on the behavior for which the rewards were given."[1] These people suggest that some kinds of praise may do more harm than good.

Too much praise or praise for mediocre performance. This praise can leave children wondering whether you have lower standards than they do. An adult friend recalls, "Mother told us all the time that we were wonderful. Anything we did was terrific. She gushed over our art, our cooking, any chores we did. But we knew that some things we had done weren't really that great. After a while we began to wonder if *any* of it was. How could we tell?"

Robert Barnes says, "There's a difference between loving your child simply because it's your child and praising a child for doing something well. Love comes automatic, praise has to do with doing a good job."

Praise that sets up the parent as the final authority on what constitutes a "good" job. This form of praise can "lead to dependency because children come to rely on the authority figure to tell them what is right or wrong, good or bad."[2] By using value words like "good" or "great" to evaluate a finished product, the parent says "I know what terrific is" but doesn't give the child a clue about what the criteria are. A child who consistently receives praise of this type may expect someone else to determine what is good and what is not.

A more effective way to say the same thing is to tell the child something you notice, "I see that the lavatory really sparkles since you cleaned it," or to ask the child to evaluate the job, "Do you feel proud of getting the bathroom so clean?"

Praise for jobs that anyone can do well. This kind of praise makes children feel that parents think they are capable of very little. Children who are praised for doing a good job washing dishes in a family where everyone washes dishes may wonder if their parents think that's all they can do. When my sons played baseball, it did *not* make them feel better to strike out and be told they had swung well. "Swinging well doesn't cut it," one snarled. "Some guys swing well *and* hit the ball."

Praise for doing something the child already finds rewarding. Praise in this situation can make that activity less intrinsically motivating.[3] A talented artist who trained as a professional illustrator found the work empty. She said, "When I was small, I loved art, and was pretty good at it. The one thing my parents always praised me for was art. My sister was cute and funny, but I was always 'the artist.' After a while I didn't do art because I loved art, I did it to get their praise. Now, if I don't get verbal and enthusiastic praise, I don't like doing it." Fortunately she was able, eventually, to recapture her love of doing art for art's sake, but her story speaks to us who are tempted to praise our children for doing what they already enjoy.

Maria Montessori also warned against praising a child who is in the middle of a task, for praise distracts a working child.

OFFERING EFFECTIVE PRAISE

So how can we praise a child who does do a good job? Early childhood specialists suggest these ways to give effective praise or encouragement.

Praise for something specific. Don't say, "You did a great job," which is vague and implies that the parent is an authority on what a great job is but, "I noticed that you took a lot of care in doing your work" or "I saw how carefully you polished the tables" or "You really used your head in the way you did that chore."

Praise with sincerity. Praise only genuine progress or accomplishment, and speak in a natural voice, not a falsely enthusiastic one. "Fake praise is recognized as such by children. Look in a child's eyes and praise only when you really see hard work. Avoid speaking in a sing-song, saccharine voice."[4]

A WISE PARENT KNOWS:
A *word aptly spoken*
is like apples of gold
in settings of silver.

Proverbs 25:11

Praise more often in private than in public. Children know when we are praising them primarily to motivate their brothers and sisters to follow their "good" example.

Focus praise on progress, not product. Sometimes children are genuinely unaware of how well they have done. We help them know when we ask, "Did you notice that you didn't spill a single drop of water when you did dishes tonight?"

Give praise that helps a child evaluate his or her own work. "You really got the floors cleaner this week. What made the difference?" "I want seconds on that cake. How did you make it taste so good?"

Praise in nonverbal ways. Show with a hug or a touch that you recognize your child has done a good job.

THE PAY-FOR-WORK VS. ALLOWANCE DEBATE

Almost everyone agrees that children need to learn to handle money responsibly. Most families provide money one way or another. But should that money come as a regular allowance or as wages for chores?

"Do *not* pay children for doing chores!" says John Rosemond unequivocally. He argues that doing so will create the illusion that if children don't want money they are not obligated to do chores. Further, it dilutes the learning experience because work that is paid for isn't done for the sake of making a contribution to the family. "Paying for chores . . . may teach a child something about business, but nothing about the responsibility that accompanies membership in a family."[5]

Robert Barnes agrees. "I think it is ludicrous to pay children to be a family member. I do not get paid to empty the dishwasher, nor do I pay them to do it. Paying for every chore only leads to further arguments: 'I'm older now, so I should get more for doing this job,' or, if you ask them to bring in garbage cans from the curb, 'How much will you give me for doing that?'

"I also think that paying children for every chore makes them 'unministryable,' to create a word. When the old man down the street needs something done, they won't do it for the sake of helping someone out, but because they want money."

Parents say: "I don't feel a child should be paid for doing what he or she is supposed to do as part of the family." "Children need to learn to work for work's sake and because it needs to be done, without being paid for it." "We want them to understand that work in the family is something that is needed. All family members have to contribute their share for the family to be in good shape."

On the other side of the debate, financial counselor Larry Burkett argues that giving children an allowance without tying it to chores doesn't realistically mirror the world they will one day have to live and work in. Adults work for pay, he points out, and children should learn that money comes from work, not merely from existence. Citing Proverbs 16:26, "The laborer's appetite works for him," Burkett argues that while a child ought not be paid for cleaning his or her own room or picking up toys, work that is for the entire family ought to be compensated—just as parents get paid for working on behalf of the entire family at outside jobs.[6]

It comes as no surprise that children agree with Burkett. Children know that adults get paid for what they do—and that entertainment and sports heroes get paid plenty. Their older friends and siblings earn money for working at restaurants, clothing stores, and grocery stores. "If housework, yardwork, and baby-sitting is all the work we can do before we're fifteen," they argue, "then we ought to get paid for doing it."

As we saw earlier, research suggests that children don't regard housework as "real work." When young children see their older siblings getting paid at restaurants—especially if older siblings are excused from housework once they get "paying jobs"—the younger kids may conclude: housework is not as important as other work; I would rather do other work.

Some families that don't pay children for doing housework—traditionally women's work—do pay for mowing the lawn—traditionally a man's job. Many who pay for both pay a far larger hourly wage for the lawn than for work inside the house. What is that teaching? If we say we pay more for mowing because mowing is harder work, how do we explain to children why office executives make more than ditch diggers and farm workers?

In my own interviews, mothers who work outside the home, especially single mothers, were more likely to base their children's income on chores. Sandy said wryly, "What motivates my children to do chores? Basically, money!"

It's tempting to conclude that employed women who have experienced both what it feels like to get paid for your work *and* what it feels like to do housework all day for no pay, have decided to share with their children the joys of getting paid. In some cases, single mothers depend heavily on children to do household chores. Linda said, "My daughter does nearly all our housework, and I pay her just as I would anyone I hired. She knows what she has to do and that she won't get paid until she does it. She has to buy her own clothes for the most part, so she really wants the money. She even asks if she can do extra work to earn more."

WHAT'S THE BEST WAY?

If we parents want to raise responsible, ministering children and if we want our children to learn to manage money, what shall we make of this controversy?

Once again, it seems to me that every family has to decide for itself how to reward children for work: give an outright allowance, pay only for chores, or devise a combination of the two.

Conversations with children reveal that they don't see as much difference as their parents do between paying for chores or giving an allowance and assigning chores—especially in families that withhold children's allowance if chores aren't done.

As your family discusses these issues, you may want to consider these values:

1. *The value of developing skills.* All children need to learn to do household tasks. Even children raised in a home with paid household help may see a day when the family fortune is lost.

2. *The value of caring for one's own needs.* Children need to learn to take care of their own rooms, clothes, toys.

3. *The value of being a part of the family.* Children, like adults, need to have some jobs they do simply because they belong to the family—maybe jobs that are frequent and equally needed by everyone, like cooking or dishes. The family may want to do major cleanups together.

4. *The value of serving others.* The best way to teach children the joy and value of serving others is to set an example and do it as a family. Our sons and I went weekly one summer to a homeless shelter to provide arts and crafts for children whose parents were out looking for work. Another family shares its thanksgiving dinner with lonely people. A third family shovels snow for elderly neighbors. A fourth cleans its grandmother's house on a regular basis. Children learn to minister to others as they do it *and* as they see their parents do it joyfully.

5. *The value of sharing the responsibility for keeping the house clean.* Each family needs to decide what work, regular and occasional, is necessary to maintain the house. Then the family needs to decide who will do what as well as what jobs will be rewarded with pay.

6. *The value of being paid for honest labor.* Children, like adults, like to be paid for work. This may be for all work, some work, or just big jobs.

Some jobs lend themselves to "extra pay" in many families: weeding, baby-sitting, growing vegetables to sell, cleaning out refrigerators, cleaning ovens, mopping and waxing floors, bleaching mildewed lawn sets and shower stalls, washing cars.

A family that normally hires outsiders (housecleaning services, lawn services, window cleaners, etc.) can pay children to do any work a paid outsider would normally do.

HOW DIFFERENT FAMILIES PAY

Once a family decides what chores will and will not be rewarded with pay, one more question arises: How much should we pay?

Few families are going to pay minimum wage to children. But we should offer trained children more than just nickels and dimes for jobs that would cost us many dollars if they were done by a professional. Consider two factors when setting wages: how much money the family has to spend and how much money the child needs to earn.

In one family the parents calculated how much they were giving their children for movies, snacks, toys, school events, and camps, and they based the amount they would pay their children on what they normally gave them anyway.

Richard and Linda Eyre, co-authors of *Teaching Children Responsibility*, pay their daughter for practicing music, which they view as a chore.[7] She gets a certain amount for each day she practices, and the amount is increased if she practices every day for a week without being reminded. The child uses the money to buy clothes.

The Eyres argue that their own outlay of money is exactly the same as before, but by tying the money to her practice, they teach the child that what she has to spend on clothes is directly tied to her responsible behavior: practicing the piano.

If it's helpful to have some idea of how and what other families pay, let me share with you what I heard:

Some families divide work into big jobs and small jobs and pay a rate for each: for school-age children, $1.00–$1.50 for big jobs and $.50–$.75 for small ones; for preschoolers, $.05–$.10 for small jobs and $.10–$.50 for large ones. Older preschoolers do more and earn more per job than three-year-olds.

Some families pay a flat rate per room, ranging from $1.50–$2.50.

In some families, children choose how many jobs they want to do based on how much they want to earn. In others, the children are told how many chores they must do for their fair share.

In some families the children each have a chore list and are paid a flat weekly rate for doing all the chores. The most common figure was $5.00 per week for older children and teens who work up to three hours a week on chores.

Madelle's family has "adult chores" and "children's chores," and the two children decide each week who will do which of the children's chores.

To get around the problem Barnes mentioned, "I don't get paid for emptying the dishwasher, neither does my child," one family pays the parents at the same rate as the children. The total family outlay/income doesn't change, but parents now have some money they have "earned" to spend as they wish.

BIG CHILD, LITTLE CHILD

Jean brought up a problem that can arise in families where children's ages are widely spaced. "Our six-year-old worked hard all week. He emptied trash cans, set the table, and fed the cats daily. He got two dollars. The twelve-year-old mowed the lawn once and got five dollars. It wasn't fair! The little one had put in more time and had to be daily responsible, yet we didn't feel we could pay for his little chores what we pay for mowing half an acre. How can we be fair?"

It *is* a problem to set prices that are fair to very different ages. Do we base them on how hard a person works, on how long a job takes, on how many times it has to be done, or on age alone? The best solution is probably a negotiated combination of all of the above.

One family has a family-allowance formula that can also be helpful in calculating prices for chores: they pay each child an allowance of $.25/week/year of age from ages two to seven; $.50/week/year of age from eight to fifteen, and $1.00/week/year of age from ages sixteen to eighteen. So a six-year-old would receive $1.50/week and a twelve-year-old would receive $6.00/week. As income grows, so does the list of responsibilities to be done and the list of what the allowance must pay for: little ones have few chores and pay out only a tithe and money for small treats; older ones pay a tithe, a regular amount to savings, and money for their own toys, movies, and special treats; teens even help pay for their clothing.

Parents who want to pay for chores rather than giving an allowance or in addition to an allowance might use those amounts as guidelines and assign chore prices by difficulty—but making certain that *all* ages work at the same frequency (daily or weekly) and have the same number of chores. Larger children do harder chores and get paid more; little ones know that when they are older and able to do those chores, they will be paid more for doing them.

YOU GET A PRIZE!

Some families offer rewards that have nothing to do with money. Some ideas:

• Have a rotated "week off" for each family member.

- Take young children to the library or park when chores are done.
- Take a family sail or picnic when leaves are raked.
- After Saturday mornings cleaning house together, let family members take turns choosing a video and making popcorn for a family Saturday evening, as well.
- Ice cream outings, family games, trips to the park, trips to a secondhand bookstore, and having a friend over for the night were rewards that children suggested they like to get.

Obviously rewards become bribes if they must get bigger and bigger to be effective, and they become ho-hum if every chore is followed by a reward. Usually, however, as children become accustomed to doing chores, they need less praise, money, and other rewards for doing them.

SUMMARY

When I was a little girl, my grandmother taught me you get more flies with honey than with vinegar. That's true in this context too. Children who are rewarded *with something they value* are more likely to take up household chores without grumbling. As they begin to see their work as needed by the family, the rewards can diminish.

Their work *is* needed at home. It can be very useful in your workplace too. Let's consider a few possibilities.

CHAPTER TWELVE

Take Your Children to Work

MY "LEGALLY ADULT" birthday came a few days too late for me to vote in one presidential election, but that fall I volunteered to help my preferred candidate each week. "We're sorry, but we don't have any work for you," I was told. "Somebody donated an old mimeograph machine, but nobody knows how to use it." As I ran my eyes over that ancient machine, my eyes sparkled. I knew how to use it. It was just like one I helped my father run bulletins on until I was twelve.

Growing up in a home where for many years Dad's office was at one end of the house, my sister and I took it for granted that we would fold, stuff, lick, and stamp church mailings, run off and fold bulletins, and answer the phone for church calls. We learned to meet deadlines, do neat work, work office equipment, meet people and make them welcome, and function in adult life situations. A friend still remembers her surprise that in high school I already knew how to greet people and accept food donations for a bereaved family. My sister, now a banker, attributes her love for office routine to helping out in Dad's office.

As we saw in our earlier look at the history of children and work, children for centuries learned to function in the adult world by working beside parents or employers. Modern children, however, seldom experience the adult workplace until they themselves are adults.

I think that's a shame. Let's bring back child labor!

Obviously I'm not suggesting that children return to factories, mills, slaughterhouses, and chimneys or that they be forced to labor eight and ten hours a day to support their families. On the other hand, in our zeal to correct very real abuses, we have forgotten a reality that made those abuses possible: children can do many productive, useful parts of adult work as well as adults can—and they can learn from doing it.

WHAT CAN CHILDREN DO?

We are all familiar with children as baby-sitters and mowers of lawns, but children are capable of many other things:

The evening before I wrote this chapter, David helped me get out a bulk mailing. He folded, collated, stapled, labeled, and sorted letters by zip code.

In a former office, a secretary's child of six helped me sort files alphabetically. He *loved* practicing his alphabet!

A seven-year-old spent a happy morning dusting and reshelving books in her uncle's home office.

By the time they are nine, children can file as well as most adults—and better than some. They can answer phones, sort mail, collate and staple reports, proofread, and make copies. A nine-year-old we knew was delighted whenever he was asked to run *big* jobs on the copier.

When one small office moved, the boss's thirteen-year-old son was their most careful packer and carrier of boxes.

Barbara's father was sales manager for a seed company. "He hired me sometimes for seventy-five cents an hour to do filing or help with other office work."

Joshua's father managed a prestigious restaurant. From the time Josh was very small, he loved to dress in a suit and tie and show people to their table with a bow. At age nine he was greeting customers and answering the phone with poise and charm.

Two women who started a decorating business employed their children in cleaning and stuffing large pillows and helping with mailings. When their children were ages eleven and thirteen, they were taught to sew shades, dust ruffles, and table skirts. They were started at a training wage of $2.00 an hour and paid more as their skills increased.

Another woman hired a fourth-grade neighbor to watch her small fabric shop while the owner picked up a child at school each afternoon after band rehearsal. The girl was soon able not only to manage the cash register but also to measure and cut fabric.

Beth loved to answer the phone and wait on customers at her father's clothing store. By age nine she was competent to fill out charge slips, which were then approved by an adult. Her older sister Lee got a work permit on her fourteenth birthday and a week later was busily selling at the Father's Day Sale. Now, four years later, she is in college studying fashion merchandising.

We have twice had a high-school student who regularly cleaned our house. Each came once a week for four hours after school, cleaning the upstairs one week and the downstairs the next.

We also had a ten-year-old "nanny" one summer when our children were very young. She played with them every morning, fed them lunch, and put them down for their naps while I wrote a book on the front porch. If she needed me, of course, I was available, but she often kept them happy for a whole morning without my help.

Another summer a fifteen-year-old boy took our boys to a pool or played with them at home each morning, then fed them lunch.

When Barnabas was thirteen, he was hired to rake and bag oak leaves covering a large lawn down the street. He worked for six hours and had thirty-two bags by the time he was done. "I didn't know if I could finish it," he gasped, "but I told her I would, so I did!"

A man who runs a public-relations office hires his daughter to assemble press kits.

A lawyer has taught his children how to shelve books in his law-firm library.

A couple who owns a dry-cleaning business hired their sons to distribute fliers announcing the opening of their second location.

Ann's father, a farmer, hired his children to "walk the fields" chopping weeds. "It was enormously hard," she remembers, "but Dad paid us instead of somebody else, so we had money for college."

A first-grade teacher hires her middle-school children at the beginning of each season to design and put up fresh bulletin boards in her classroom. She has also begun to hire them to help her grade papers, which she checks afterward.

A writer friend pays her computer-wise son to run a spellcheck on manuscripts as well as print and assemble final copies for mailing.

The owner of a small business hires his computer-whiz daughter to run his mailing labels and do his accounts at the end of each month, then he checks her work. "She makes fewer mistakes than I used to," he grins.

I asked a representative of the U.S. Department of Labor to read this chapter for accuracy, and he informed me that many of these children were working illegally. "Only parents and companies not subject to the wage-and-hour law can legally employ children," I was told.

Yet each of those children did a responsible job in which they took pride, and none was in the least harmed by the work they did. Have we gotten far enough from the horrors of massive child labor to be ready for a new law? If not, parents can still employ their own children in businesses they own, or—although not legally—pay a child from their own pockets for occasional help.

WHY HIRE YOUR CHILD?

Look around your home and office and consider the two reasons I suggested at the beginning of this book for teaching children to work at home: children need to learn skills, and parents need help. What jobs that need doing can a child be trained to do?

Linda Stern wrote an article urging self-employed parents to involve children in their work. "Hiring your children instills in them a sense of independence, shows them the value of earning their own money, and helps them build confidence in their abilities." She finds that children who work for their parents also learn the importance of taking a task from start to finish, see their parents overcoming obstacles, get a firsthand look at the daily routine of the workplace, and come to understand better who their parents are by watching what they do.[1]

Miriam Kohn, a child psychologist, agrees. "When children work in a family business, they learn at an early age what it means to take on responsibility."[2]

In addition to the benefits for the child, parent employers also benefit. They keep the money in the family, but children pay taxes at a lower rate and may put the savings away for education.

BE A GOOD NEIGHBOR

If employing our own children is good, employing our neighbor's children may be even better. A study of children and work found that sixty-five percent of the boys and seventy percent of the girls had done their first work-for-pay for neighbors or friends of the family. The authors of the study report conclude:

> Assuming that parents do value their children's gaining outside work experiences at an early age, each may see in his neighbor the potential to play a role which, however much needs to be done at home, one cannot play for one's own child, namely that of "outside," yet known and trusted "employer." It is not difficult to imagine a set of circumstances under which norms of reciprocity evolve among neighbors regarding the salutary employment of one another's children when the opportunity presents itself. One can conceive even of the occasional "creation" of childwork in order that the

social function of introducing children to the world of work
may be carried out early, and in a "safe" environment.[3]

Doesn't that sound very much like the apostle Paul's comments in 1 Corinthians 12 about the various parts of the body working together for the good of the whole? Children need to learn to function in the adult world. They need to learn to work for adults who are not their parents, and they need to learn in safe, trusted environments. Who better than church brothers and sisters can provide what Goldstein calls "circumstances under which norms of reciprocity evolve"? Can we in the church serve those functions for one another's children?

There are several advantages to hiring other people's children and letting them hire ours. First, children often give their best effort for someone else. Our son never worked as hard at home as he did for the woman who hired him to rake and bag leaves. After he dragged home red-faced, weary, and satisfied, neither he nor we will ever wonder again whether he can be a hard, diligent worker.

A second advantage of hiring other people's children is that parents don't all have the same skills or interests. A child who works in a variety of settings may develop interests and abilities their parents don't have. When my sister was in high school, she worked in a church member's biology lab. While I was in college, I worked in a church member's insurance office, and a boy who would one day be an army colonel helped the church secretary and learned what it takes to manage an office.

How many of us parents got our first "real pay" from someone we knew? Do we have work that children of our friends and neighbors could do?

Imagine a group of Christian friends who covenanted to hire one another's children. Imagine a church-school class or whole congregation that set up a committee to hire interested children from the church in a variety of working situations. What benefits could those children reap—not only from learning skills but also from working with older Christian role models?

Tips for Hiring a Child or Young Teen

When hiring children—your own or someone else's—use these suggestions to make the working relationship easier:

1. Take them and their work seriously. Be businesslike.

2. Make certain they agree to do the work.

3. Together set up a fair wage or reward.

4. Teach carefully the job they are to do.

5. If they are to work regularly rather than occasionally, draw up a written contract stating expectations and wages.

6. Set a payday and stick to it. Don't pay in advance and nag for undone work, and don't expect work for which you promise to pay "later."

7. Schedule specific times for work to be done and stick to them.

8. If the job takes a long time, be sure the child knows to take a break. Some children will work right through lunch hour because they are shy about asking if they can rest.

9. Teach that earning is both fun and rewarding. Expect your own child to both spend some money and save some.

10. Separate home and work. Don't punish at home for job infractions, or vice versa.

A WORD OF CAUTION

The Fair Labor Act was partially designed "to protect the educational opportunities of minors and prohibit their employment in jobs and under conditions detrimental to their health or well-being." It outlines who may legally hire children—and for what.

This law applies to any business that is engaged in interstate commerce and to businesses earning more than $500,000 a year. It doesn't cover parents who employ their own children in a solely owned business not engaged in interstate commerce or a solely owned business not making $500,000 or more a year.

During the school year, the law permits fourteen- and fifteen-year-olds to be employed for up to three hours a day after school and up to eighteen hours a week in a variety of jobs except mining, manufacturing, or hazardous jobs. However, they *may* work in a non-hazardous job in those fields. Under the law, children under age fourteen can deliver papers, work as baby-sitters and actors, or work in family businesses as described above.

Before you hire any young person—unless you own a business and plan to hire your own child to work in it—you should read "Child Labor Requirements in Nonagricultural Occupations Under the Fair Labor Standards Act," available free from the U.S. Department of Labor office in your state. You may also want to check state regulations.

One set of parents described earlier paid their daughters a "training wage" at first. Since laws about training and student wages will have changed before this book goes to press, prospective employers interested in paying student-learners a training wage should consult the Wage-Hour Office for up-to-date information.

MONEY'S NOT THE ONLY PAY

When I asked David to help with my mailing, I asked him, "How much would you charge me?"

He considered it seriously. "Buy me a big book, Mama, one big enough to glue pages together and make a box to keep things in." He added, with a child's shrewdness, "Money's not the only kind of pay, you know."

That's a good thing. While legally any worker covered under the wage-and-hour law is supposed to be paid stipulated wages, regardless of age, few children under age fourteen are worth the adult minimum wage—and few of us are willing to pay workers more than they are worth. How do we, then, compensate a child?

Children under the age of fourteen may agree eagerly to trade labor for something besides money: fast-food coupons, video rentals, trips to the movies, merchandise from the store in which they are working, or credits toward buying something they want. The child who minded the fabric store was paid in remnants and given sewing lessons. Once when we moved into a huge house that needed a lot of scrubbing and yardwork, I promised neighborhood children a day at an amusement park for their help. I got more helpers than I needed!

Please don't misunderstand: I'm not advocating the exploitation of children. I'm advocating that creative adults find ways to teach children workplace skills whenever possible and pay them in something that the children themselves value.

Paying in something other than money will not, of course, teach a child how to budget or help that child contribute toward education, but it can be a way to start a child very early in working hard for others and learning to take responsibility for doing good work.

SUMMARY

Consider your home or office. What jobs there can your own child or someone else's do? Hiring a child or young adult can benefit both you and the child.

CHAPTER THIRTEEN

Is It Ever Too Late?

"**I** WISH WE'D HAD that book fifteen years ago," a friend responded when I told him what I was working on. "Our grown son has just moved back home. We didn't expect much from him when he was growing up, and now it's too late."

Is it?

Maybe not.

I haven't yet had children who wanted to move back home, since my own children haven't yet *left* home, but I've learned a lot both from my own experience as a young adult who moved back home and from twenty young adults who have lived with Bob and me for weeks or months, sharing meals and household chores.

After college, my parents gave me the option of returning home for a year to save money so I could go to Scotland to write. They made it clear at the beginning, however, that some things would be different. First, I would pay a weekly sum for room and board—off the top of my earnings, not "if I had anything left over." I would be responsible for some cooking, cleaning, and my own laundry, and—for the first time in my life—I would have a curfew.

"If I'm going to be able to teach school each day," my mother told me, "I need my sleep. When you stay out late, I automatically lie awake until you get home. Since you'll be here during the school year, you will need to be in each night by twelve."

"I'm twenty-one!" I protested. "You don't need to lie awake."
"But I *do* lie awake," she replied, "and I can't teach the next day without enough sleep." My parents reminded me that I didn't have to live at home, but if I chose to, I would have to abide by the rules. That was only fair.

That winter we began the process of relating to one another as adults-to-adult, a relationship I still cherish.

WHY PARENTS DON'T MAKE YOUNG ADULTS WORK

When young adults return to live in their parents' home as the children they once were—expecting a room, a car to drive, insurance coverage, food on the table three times a day, a place to entertain friends, and few responsibilities—it is usually not the children but the *parents* who permit this to happen. Why? Consider these possible reasons:

1. *The Perennial Parent.* "I don't mind doing the extra work. All I ever wanted to be was a mother."

Some parents—especially some mothers—find their major reason for living in their parenthood. A child moving back home means that they again get to cook meals, clean and do laundry, and support the child with money and concern. But these parents sacrifice their children's maturity and future on the altar of their own need to be needed. Only by seeking to find out what else they have been created to be and do—and sharing some family responsibilities—can they move their children toward mature adulthood.

2. *The Indulgent Parent.* "My kids are too busy to help around the house. Besides, it's fun having them around. They and their friends keep me young."

Children whom we enjoy *are* fun to have around. They pop in and out, fill the house with music and friends, provide companionship, and generally pep us up. Letting them live a carefree, irresponsible existence at home may express our delight in having them around—but is it good for them?

Read again in chapter one what counselors and personnel directors say about the chances an irresponsible, carefree adult has of functioning well in marriage and the world of work. Do we care enough about them to steer them into disciplined acceptance of responsibilities, including household chores?

3. *The Powerless Parent.* "I can't *make* her work. I can't even get her to hang up her clothes, much less do family laundry."

These parents always thought it was too much hassle to teach their children household chores. Now, frustrated and weary, they wish they could "make" the child share household chores. They expect—and may get—rebellion, resentment, procrastination, and all the resistances we looked at earlier when they try.

We have lived with some young adults unaccustomed to work and discovered that since they have a high value on their own comfort, it's possible to motivate them by creating discomfort. Consider again what chapter ten said about teaching through consequences.

The most drastic—and logical—consequence for a grown child, of course, is, "If you don't abide by the rules, you move out." But milder consequences can make life just uncomfortable enough to make a grown child agree to work.

- Natural consequences: "If you don't clear your place at the table, you'll have dirty dishes at the next meal." "If you don't do your own laundry, you won't have clothes to wear." "If you don't take your turn cooking for the others, we won't take our turn cooking for you."
- Related consequences: "If you don't pay your share, you'll get no meals." "If you don't look for a job, you will get no gas money and your car insurance will be cancelled."
- Imposed consequences: "If you don't do your fair share of cleaning, your car will be impounded." "If you break a family item and don't replace it, your possessions may be impounded and possibly sold to pay the damages."

Powerless parents usually haven't set *and enforced* consequences in the past. They may be amazed at results if they do!

4. *The Rescuing Parent.* "If my kid is asked to help around the
house or if I don't let him stay out as late as he likes, he'll move in
with his friends. They are a terrible influence on him. I'd rather do
all the work than have him living with them."

Some children make their parents desperate to have them
leave yet manage to stay home for years messing up the house,
spending their parents' money, eating their parents' food, and
giving absolutely nothing in return. Why?

"Parental fear," says my husband, who has counseled both
parents and the children. "They have blackmailed their parents into
believing that if they don't give the children everything they want,
the children will leave home and get into terrible, even life-
threatening trouble, like promiscuity and drugs. The parents' love
for their children makes them hostages to the children. They are
ultimately afraid their children can't make it without them."

Granted the world can be a scary place, with life-threatening
dangers. On the other hand, immaturity is also a life-threatening
danger. These children, of all children, need desperately to begin to
learn skills for adulthood. Can their parents be brave enough to
insist that they do?

Counseling or support groups may be necessary to make
grown children willing to learn—or to make parents willing to do
the tough-love things that can teach them. Often patterns of
dealing with anger and frustration have to be changed by both
parents and children. It's hard, but supporting and caring for an
immature child all your life will be much harder!

HOW DO WE BEGIN?

Parents who permit a grown child to move back home need to
see this as a new beginning, not merely a continuing of "the way
we were." Both parents and child have changed since the child
moved away. The child has tasted independence, grown accus-

tomed to making his or her own decisions without justifying them to parents, may be earning money or seeking a job. The parents may have adjusted their household, budget, schedule, and lifestyle too. Some parents have also begun to think about "What I wish I'd taught that child before he or she left."

Begin by relating to your child as an adult you can reason with and listen to. And call a family meeting!

When Bob and I have given or rented rooms to young adults, we have found that it's always wise to work out a contract of expectations that all of us can agree to. When we have, we've had a smooth and pleasant household. When we haven't, we've had bruised feelings on both sides and occasional real storms.

WHAT IF MY GROWN CHILD "DOESN'T WANT TO"?

Children usually move back home for two reasons. One group has tried the adult world, has made some mistakes, and comes home to recover. The second group comes home to save on living expenses. Many of both kinds will expect to shoulder a fair share of family responsibilities.

Some children who have been wounded, however, will expect to lick their wounds indefinitely while you provide lots of sympathy and full care. And some children who want to save on expenses will expect to enjoy an extended childhood and use their income to buy expensive adult toys—fancy cars, electronic gadgets, expensive clothes, and vacations. Some, especially grown sons, even expect their parents' home to function as a cheap or free motel, where they can come and go as they please with no accountability or responsibility.

All these children need your shelter and food. They also desperately need any help you can give them toward maturing.

Be honest with your feelings, your own needs, and your limits with this living arrangement. State your expectations as well as the consequences of failing to meet those expectations. Don't be

---

Tips for a Family Meeting with Grown Children

1. Before you call a meeting, look over "Guidelines for a Family Meeting" in chapter five.

2. Start the first meeting by giving each person time to describe how things are different from when the child was growing up at home.

3. Discuss: "What has to be done to make this new arrangement work for all of us? What is a fair way to run our new household?" You may need to use the "Fairness Approach to Family Conflict" in chapter nine.

4. Consider together everything that has to be done to maintain the home with this new person added. Who will be responsible for each job? What areas of conflict do you anticipate? Because you are all adults now, the guidelines for developing a family style in chapter four may be helpful.

5. Draw up a "Contract of Expectations" (see next page). Post it conspicuously.

6. If your child hasn't learned all the "Personal Skills a Child Needs to Learn" in chapter six, decide when you will teach what.

7. Set a date to evaluate your new living arrangement. You may even want to set a tentative date and schedule for the child to move away from home.

---

blackmailed by pity or fear into treating grown children like infants. Grit your teeth and remind yourself every day: "It is time this child grew up"!

If you are tempted to keep them children—or feel "mean" for asking them to take a share of household responsibilities— remember: strolling mockingbirds and irresponsible adults don't

Guidelines for a Contract of Expectations
Between Parents and Young Adult Children

1. How much money will the young adults contribute to the household? When will it be paid?

2. If the young adults are unemployed, what will they do for the household to "earn" their keep? What do the young adults need to do to show in earnest that they are seeking employment?

3. If a grandchild is involved, who will care for the child? Who will support the child? If grandparents must contribute financially to the child's support, what will the young adult do in exchange (additional housework, yardwork)?

4. What responsibilities will the young adult accept for cooking, dishes, cleaning, and yardwork? Draw up a month's Chore Chart.

5. What other rules need to be set? Possibilities include curfews, use of bathroom, use of telephone, entertainment of guests of both sexes, use of radio or musical instruments, snacks, where food will be eaten, kitchen cleanup, garbage take-out, how the young adult's room shall be maintained and by whom. One family even drew up a plan for where boxes were to be stored while the young adult was moving back in, and when the boxes were to be emptied and removed.

6. What are the consequences for infractions of these rules? Do all parties agree to accept those consequences?

survive in the real world. If your children aren't maturing at twenty-two, they aren't likely to become magically mature at forty.

This is a new season in both your lives. It offers a chance for you to teach—without long sermons and "I told you so's"—some things your child badly needs to learn.

SUMMARY

When young adult children move home, it's time for a whole new set of rules. Now they can be treated like adults—just as they would be treated in someone else's home or just as you would treat any other adult with whom you agree to share your home. The beauty of a child's moving back is that you get a chance to begin to build an adult-to-adult relationship with a very special person: your own child.

Living with young adults can be a pleasant, enjoyable time of building a new kind of relationship between parents and child, or it can be a nightmare.

It's *your* house. And it *your* choice. Which will it be?

CHAPTER FOURTEEN

Why We Parents Have To

"**T**RAIN A CHILD in the way he should go," declares Proverbs 22:6, "and when he is old he will not turn from it."

Is that true? Do we really need to worry about training our children? Is it not enough to educate them, feed them well, keep them healthy and safe from danger, and set them a good personal example?

Probably not.

The term "train" doesn't mean to correct errors but to teach to become capable. We potty train children. Athletes are trained to compete. Training involves doing something over and over again until it is mastered, both on days when the trainee feels like doing it and on days when the trainee would rather goof off.

WHAT HAPPENS IF WE DON'T?

What happens to children who are not trained? The Bible gives us one excellent—and sad—illustration. Picture David, King of Israel, sitting in the palace with his sons, telling stories about "When I was a little boy."

"Boys, I had to work *hard*! My father sent me out with the sheep from the time I was small. I had to sleep near them, fight lions and bears, tramp all over the countryside looking for green pastures and still waters.

"When war broke out, your grandfather Jesse sent me miles away to take my big brothers food, and I had to go on foot—none of this riding donkeys, Absalom. We had to *walk* when we wanted to go anywhere. But living rough was good for me. I could never have survived all those years hiding from King Saul's armies if I hadn't learned how to live outdoors and by my wits. I could never have killed Goliath if I hadn't had to fight bears and lions. I didn't have time to flirt with pretty women, Amnon.

"And you, Solomon, complain about practicing your alphabet? Let me tell you about practicing! I had to practice every day on the harp. But by the time I was a teenager, I was good enough to play for King Saul himself."

David's father and mother may have originated the family proverb about training up a child. They certainly provided opportunities for him to mature. As an adult, David continued to be responsible, righteous (with one lapse), concerned for his family, disciplined, hardworking, and devoted to God.

Like many parents who mature through a rigorous childhood, however, David gave his children a softer life. Raised in a palace with few responsibilities, Amnon and Absalom grew up thinking they should have anything they wanted. They each died a horrible death as a direct result of that faulty thinking.

Solomon was given the kingdom, but he was not well trained for adulthood. Consider, for instance, what David says and does in 1 Chronicles 22:5–6: "David said, 'My son Solomon is young and inexperienced, and the house to be built for the Lord should be of great magnificence and fame and splendor in the sight of all the nations. Therefore I will make preparations for it.' So *David* made extensive preparations before his death. *Then* he called for his son Solomon and charged him to build a house for the Lord, the God of Israel" (italics added).

Instead of calling Solomon in to help him plan the temple and order supplies, David made extensive preparations himself, then handed the project over. David did *for* instead of *with* his son. He never laid on him the responsibility—and chances to mature— that Jesse had provided David himself.

What kind of man did Solomon become? He was materialistic, lacking his father's delight in the simple joys of nature; wise in governing, but without his father's compassion and temperance; devoted to his work rather than to his family; often married, but with no hint of the parental love that tore David apart at Absalom's death; dedicated to pleasure; eventually so jaded that he declared, "Everything is vanity under the sun." He was religious, but he never developed the deep faith that was the core of David's being, providing both counsel and rebuke. What a contrast Solomon's writings are to the joy, zest for life, praise, and dependence on God contained in his father's psalms!

Materialistic, wise in his business but not in family life, outwardly religious, often married, pleasure seeking—does that sound like anybody we know? Solomon is any child who is not trained in "the way s/he should go." But while Solomon doesn't seem to have either benefited from or followed that advice with his own sons, we can be grateful he passed it on to us.

A child is not trained by schools, by reading books, by talking with friends, or even by life itself. Training happens at home. It requires dedication and consumes time. It can't be hurried. It is woven day by day on the loom of family life.

THE COURAGE NOT TO BE PERFECT

Before you start feeling guilty for what you have or haven't done as a parent, take comfort. If a child is living at home, *it's never too late to begin*.

But begin we must.

Our children need to know how to live and function as productive members of a family. They need to be able to care for their personal needs. They need to know how to work on a team— in the home, in the office, and in society at large. They need to know how to be accountable, responsible, and willing to work hard when necessary. They need the self-esteem of knowing they are capable. They need to know how to serve others in a selfless way, whether or not they always feel like it.

When I told one woman what this book was about, she exclaimed, "You are scaring me to death!"

I don't want to scare you to death. I do want to spur you to action.

And as you train your children, remember: our children have not only earthly imperfect parents, but a heavenly perfect Parent. We can trust God to assist us in the training. Ephesians 3:15 tells us that every family on earth is "named" by God. "To name" means to give something reality, life, purpose. Your home is God's chosen laboratory for one or more of his young children to learn basic life skills they need in order to survive. God chose *you*—whoever you are and whatever you are like—as the very best earthly parent your child or children could have. Now it's up to you, with God's help, to decide how you can best make adults out of them.

We won't, of course, be good or successful parents all the time. To train a child, we have to explore not only our child's character but also our own. We have to confront our own personal rigidities and parental flabbiness. We have to stretch our imaginations and our patience.

We won't all train our children the same way either. Parents are explorers on uncharted seas. Nobody has ever before raised our unique children in our particular families. I hope this book has given you a bit of courage to decide that it's okay if your schedule isn't like your parents' or your rules just like the ones next door. Teach your children the best things you know about life and how to live it.

Dianne, whose children are grown, speaks of the joy she feels when she looks at them now. "Today I see in my grown sons good things that I know I have sown seeds for—ways they behave and handle responsibility, things they do with their own children, things they make for their homes, the way they take pride in helping to keep the home. In them, I can see myself. That's a terrific reward for any parent."

Maria Montessori regarded the child as "a great external grace which enters the family." Isn't that wonderful?

God gives us our children not only for their sakes but also for our own. A parent who teaches a child to be independent, capable, and caring will have to grow up a bit in the process. At the end of our parenting years, both our children and we parents should be a little more what God intended us to be.

APPENDIX: *People Who Shared*

Robert Barnes is a marriage and family counselor and director of Sheridan House, a ministry to troubled families around Fort Lauderdale, Florida. Sheridan House provides a residential program for teenagers as well as counseling and social services to their families. Referrals to the program come from the court system, guidance counselors, and pastors. This ministry is in the budgets of ninety-two churches from fourteen denominations. Dr. Barnes did his undergraduate work at Maryville College and his graduate work at the University of Tennessee. His doctorate, from Florida Atlantic University, is in counseling. He is married and has two children, a daughter, thirteen, and a son, ten. The family shares household responsibilities.

Anne Brandon, director of the Montessori Academy of Mobile, founded the school in 1972. The Academy moved into its current facility and began an all-day program in 1985 and a program for toddlers in 1989. A native of Rochester, New York, Ms. Brandon has a bachelor's degree in music from Nazareth College, a master's degree in early childhood education from the University of South Alabama, and her Montessori training and certification from the St. Nicholas Training Center in London. She and her husband, a college professor, have three grown daughters, the oldest of whom works in the Montessori Academy. Did they all share household responsibilities? "Definitely!"

Donna Clark owns and manages Clark Personnel Services in Mobile, Alabama. The mother of four (and the very young grandmother of three), Donna has been in personnel work for twenty years. Her concern for young people was evident the first time we met, at a career-day program in our sons' high school. Her whole family shares household chores—"even my husband, and you may quote me on that. It's because they all pitch in that I have been able to achieve what I have in this business."

John Richey is Supervisor of Human Resources for the Mobile division of Alabama Power Company. He has been involved in personnel work for twenty-three years. He and his wife have one daughter in college and one in high school.

The following parents are quoted by name and sometimes anonymously to preserve their ability to speak freely:

Ann grew up on an Illinois farm with her three brothers. She is in her mid-thirties, married, currently completing her Ph.D. in Michigan while her husband also completes a degree. Because their two children are very young, we primarily discussed her own childhood work experiences.

Barbara, an ordained minister from Washington, has two sons, ages fourteen and eleven. Currently she is taking a break after years of full-time work as co-director of a working farm and Christian conference center. Her husband manages an orchard that has been in his family for four generations. The family shares household responsibilities—"with great inconsistency!"

Carol, a nurse, is the oldest of four. Her dad died when she was nine, so her mother finished her education and started teaching— first in the U.S., then in a mission school in Honduras. Carol went with her for eighth grade, then lived with grandparents and in a dorm in Illinois during high school. She is married to a software engineer, and they are raising five children, ages five to seventeen. Most of the time they also keep a foster child, and Carol works ten hours a week in a hospital. Soon after we finished this interview, the entire family went for a year to Niger to work in a mission hospital directed by Carol's uncle. This family shares household responsibilities. They have to!

Dianne grew up in New York State with one brother, who's six years younger than she. Her mother went to work when Dianne was in her early teens. At eighteen, Dianne married a member of the Coast Guard. She had her first son at nineteen and two more in the next four years. Her fourth was born when the oldest was nine. Because her husband's career required frequent moves, Dianne focused on creating a stable home for the family and worked only sporadically, most often as a church secretary. Her oldest son is now thirty, her youngest twenty-one. When the older boys were at home, they shared household responsibilities. Since they left, Dianne cares for the home.

Donna, the youngest of three children, grew up in Ohio with childhood responsibilities. Now she works as a midwife in a private group practice, and her husband is an emergency-room nurse. They share household responsibilities, and their son, five, already makes his bed, takes dishes to the sink, and picks up his toys. "He also makes breakfast if Mom's not up fast enough. Yesterday it was graham crackers and honey—just like the picture on the box. Argh!"

Dorothy grew up in an Alabama city, the seventh of fourteen children. Her parents both worked, and the children had responsibility for the home. After high school Dorothy attended one year of college, then went to work to support herself. She was married for seven years, has two children (ages thirteen and fifteen), and has been divorced for twelve years. Several years ago she became very ill and moved back in with her parents. After her father's death, she remained with her mother. The doctors told her in 1987 that she has a crippling lung condition, but currently she is in school, learning to be a tailor. "I'm looking for a better life. I'm not going to let my handicap handicap me. It's no excuse not to get on with life!" She is raising her children "as my parents raised me—to work hard."

Jean is the second of two daughters. Her father was a minister, her mother a teacher. She had some household responsibilities as a child. She married a career military non-commissioned officer who is now retired and works for an insurance company. They have three children, ages nineteen, fifteen, and eight. Jean taught history until her second child was born, was at home for four years, then began a career as a financial analyst for a trust company. As she says in one comment, she finds it difficult for several reasons to involve children in household responsibilities.

Judy is the second of six children. Since the family had traditional roles for boys and girls and Judy's only sister is sixteen years younger than she, Judy was the only child expected to help with housework until she married at age eighteen. Now a medical librarian in Alabama and the mother of two sons, she expects them to help with household responsibilities.

Linda grew up in Alaska. Her father left when she was an infant, and her mother stayed home and brought up the children. Linda has one sister, three years older, and a brother, six years older. Now Linda is a single parent with one daughter, thirteen, at home. Her son, eighteen, lives in Connecticut with his father. Her daughter does all the housework while Linda works as director of public relations for the local Goodwill Industries.

Madelle was the second of four daughters in a missionary family serving in Brazil. She grew up with few household responsibilities. She trained as a nurse, married a doctor, and stayed at home when their two children were born. When the children were thirteen and eleven, she returned to work as a nurse three days a week. The family shares household responsibilities.

Marion grew up on a farm in Alabama, the oldest of three widely spaced children—her sister was five years younger, her brother fourteen years younger. "I was essentially an only child." She has been married for over thirty years to a fireman, who is also an alcoholic. "I have had to run things, and it's my nature to try and control." They have seven children in two "clumps": the first five are now twenty-four to thirty-one; the younger two are seventeen and nineteen. Marion, now a historian and free-lance writer, worked most of the time her children were growing up. She also performed most of the household responsibilities.

Moira, a physician, was raised in New York State, the older of two sisters. Their mother was a semi-invalid, but nevertheless took care of the house; the girls helped her. Moira has been married twice, has two sons from her first marriage, and is currently divorced. Her sons are in high school and college. The family has a weekly cleaning person, but Moira insists that the boys clean their own rooms and share dishwashing responsibilities.

Norma, now in her late sixties, was raised on an Indiana farm, the youngest of five children. She and her husband had two families of three children each. "The September my oldest entered college, I had one high-school senior, one freshman, one entering first grade, one entering preschool—and a new baby!" (I should have interviewed her for my book about women and stress.) Her children worked around the house, boys outside and girls inside. They are all grown now. Norma works out of her home as a bookkeeper. She is also a former church organist.

Sandy grew up on a Massachusetts dairy farm, the third of five children. Her two sisters were older, her brothers younger than she. Her mother was at home, and the family expected the boys to work outdoors and the girls inside. Now an editor with a national publisher, Sandy has been divorced for several years and is raising a daughter, fourteen, and son, nine. Her children share the housework.

Notes

ONE: Mockingbirds Don't Stroll, Honey

1. Bernard Goldstein and Jack Oldham, *Children and Work: A Study of Socialization* (New Brunswick, N.J.: Transaction, 1979). Data derived primarily from page 74.
2. Paula Polk Lillard, *Montessori: A Modern Approach* (New York: Shocken, 1972), 115.
3. John Rosemond, *John Rosemond's Six-Point Plan for Raising Healthy, Happy Children* (New York: Andrews, McMeel, 1989), 81.
4. Frances K. Goldscheider and Linda J. Waite, *New Families, No Families: The Transformation of the American Home* (Berkeley: Univ. of Calif. Press, Studies in Demography, Series 6, 1991), quoted in "Children Help Less at Home; Dads Do More" by Barbara Vobejda, *Washington Post,* 24 November 1991: 1.
5. Goldstein and Oldham, *Children and Work,* 43, 67.
6. David and Karen Mains, *Living, Loving, Leading: Creating a Home That Encourages Spiritual Growth* (Portland, Ore.: Multnomah, 1991), 184.
7. Peter Drucker, *Management: Tasks, Responsibilities, Practices* quoted by Goldstein and Oldham, *Children and Work,* 184–85.
8. John Rosemond, *John Rosemond's Six-Point Plan for Raising Healthy, Happy Children,* 117.

TWO: Fate of Our Fathers—and Mothers

1. Barbara Kaye Greenleaf, *Children Through the Ages: A History of Childhood* (New York: McGraw-Hill, 1978), intro.
2. Mary Holbrook MacElroy, *Work and Play in Colonial Days* (New York: Macmillan, 1939). Children's chores are mentioned throughout the text.
3. Letty Cottin Pogrebin, *Growing Up Free: Raising Your Child in the '80s* (New York: McGraw-Hill, 1980), 180.
4. Greenleaf, *Children Through the Ages,* 73–74.
5. Jean Lush, "Teaching Children to Work," *Focus on the Family Magazine* (May 1991).

THREE: *Anything You Can Do, I Can Do Better!*

1. Elva Anson, *How to Get Kids to Help at Home* (New York: Ballantine, 1989), 157.
2. Jean Lush, "Teaching Children to Work," *Focus on the Family Magazine* (May 1991).
3. Patricia Sprinkle, *Women Who Do Too Much: Stress and the Myth of the Superwoman* (Grand Rapids: Zondervan, 1991), 61.
4. Paula Polk Lillard, *Montessori: A Modern Approach* (New York: Shocken, 1972), 114.

FOUR: *In My Mother's House . . .*

1. Helen Neville and Mona Halaby, *No-Fault Parenting* (New York: Facts on File Publications, 1984), 120.
2. Gretchen Hirsch, *Womanhours: A 21-Day Time Management Plan That Works* (New York: St. Martin's, 1983), 108.
3. Ibid.

FIVE: *Start with a Family Meeting*

1. Joy Berry, *Every Kid's Guide to Family Rules and Responsibilities* (Chicago: Children's Press, 1987).
2. Letty Cottin Pogrebin, *Growing Up Free: Raising Your Child in the '80s* (New York: McGraw-Hill, 1980), 179–80. The claims are hers; the replies are mine.
3. Renee Y. Magid with Nancy E. Fleming, *When Mothers and Fathers Work: Creative Strategies for Balancing Careers and Family* (New York: American Management Association, 1987), 48.
4. Ann Toland Serb and Joan Webster Anderson, *Stop the World . . . Our Gerbils Are Loose!* (Garden City: Doubleday, 1979), 21–22. A light and delightful book about parenting.
5. Pogrebin, *Growing Up Free*, 190.
6. Ibid., 191.

SIX: *Teach Skills, Not Chores*

1. Paula Polk Lillard, *Montessori: A Modern Approach* (New York: Shocken, 1972), 114.
2. Adapted from "Practical Life Album," compiled by Vicky Thompson for

the Memphis Montessori Institute, 1987. Used by permission of the author.

3. Jean Lush, "Teaching Children to Work," *Focus on the Family Magazine* (May 1991).

4. Lillard, *Montessori: A Modern Approach*, 83.

5. Eva Anson, *How to Get Kids to Help at Home* (New York: Ballantine, 1989), 40.

6. Lillard, *Montessori: A Modern Approach*, 82–83.

SEVEN: Tasks for Appropriate Age Levels

1. Jeff Campbell and The Clean Team, *Speed Cleaning* (New York: Dell, 1987).

EIGHT: Can Cleaning Be Fun?

1. James P. Comer, "Chores with a Purpose," *Parents' Magazine* (September 1989), 205.

2. Jean Lush, "Teaching Children to Work" *Focus on the Family Magazine* (May 1991).

3. Letty Cottin Pogrebin, *Growing Up Free: Raising Your Child in the '80s* (New York: McGraw-Hill, 1980), 190.

NINE: When the Troops Rebel

1. C. S. Lewis, *The Weight of Glory* (Grand Rapids: Eerdmans, 1965), 12–13. Lewis was talking about our neighbors; I altered the quotation to describe our children instead.

2. Based on Thomas Lickona, *Raising Good Children: Helping Your Child Through the Stages of Moral Development* (New York: Bantam, 1983), chap. 13.

3. Bonnie Runyon McCullough and and Susan Walker Monson, *401 Ways to Get Your Kids to Work at Home* (New York: St. Martin's, 1981), 119.

TEN: Teaching by Consequences

1. Robert Barnes, *Who's in Charge Here? Overcoming Power Struggles with Your Kids* (Dallas: Word, 1990), 5.

2. Ibid., 191.

3. Gretchen Hirsch, *Womanhours: A 21-Day Time Management Plan that Works* (New York: St. Martin's, 1983), 106.

ELEVEN: Bribing Your Kids to Work

1. Randy Hitz and Amy Driscoll, "Praise or Encouragement? New Insights into Praise," *Young Children* magazine (July 1988), 9.
2. Ibid., 8.
3. Mark Lepper, cited by Joel N. Sahurkin, "Caution: Praise Can be Destructive" *Family Learning* magazine (May/June 1984).
4. Hitz and Driscoll, "Praise or Encouragement? New Insights into Praise," 12.
5. John Rosemond, *John Rosemond's Six-Point Plan for Raising Happy, Healthy Children* (New York: Andrews and McMeel, 1989), 87.
6. Larry Burkett, *Answers to Your Family's Financial Questions* (Pomona, Ca.: Focus on the Family, 1987). The conviction that children ought to work for their income is central to all Burkett says about children and work.
7. Linda and Richard Eyre, *Teaching Children Responsibility* (New York: Ballantine Books, 1988).

TWELVE: Take Your Children to Work

1. Linda Stern, "Teach Your Kids the Value of Work," *Home Office Computing* (January 1991): 39–41.
2. Quoted by Stern, "Teach Your Kids the Value of Work," 40.
3. Bernard Goldstein and Jack Oldham, *Children and Work: A Study of Socialization* (New Brunswick, N.J.: Transaction, 1979), 77.

Children Who Do
Too Little

To the Leader

This guide is designed for a six-week study. To facilitate discussion, each participating family should have a copy of this book.

Your role is not "teacher," but group facilitator to encourage participation. To enrich class discussions, ask participants to read chapters before class. However, participants unable to prepare ahead should still be encouraged to attend and do the class exercises. If you do not complete discussion material in one session, discuss those questions in the next session or ask participants to consider the questions at home.

Remember: Each family is different, and families go through different stages. Circumstances—such as children's ages, family income, and family needs—change. There is no "one way" or "right way" for families to operate in the realm of household management. Do not let discussions get bogged down, therefore, by participants who want to impose their own slant on the entire group. Urge each group member to express opinions, and encourage the group to stay open about different family styles.

Session One

WHAT HOUSEHOLD SKILLS DO CHILDREN NEED TO LEARN—AND WHY?

BASED ON CHAPTER ONE

LEADER ADVANCE PREPARATION

Read Chapter 1 of this book and become familiar with the suggested session outline below.

Print up enough copies of the "Personal Skills" list on page 77 for participants to have one *per child* in each family. Also make sure this book is available for each family.

SUGGESTED SESSION OUTLINE

1. Beginning

Prayer. Thank God for the gift of children and ask for wisdom to bring them up in the way they should go.

Welcome. Take time for each member of the class to introduce himself or herself and say what household responsibilities he or she had as a child. Also ask each participant to describe his or her own children: names, ages, and something special about each.

Expectations. Ask each participant to complete the sentence below.

What I hope to get from this class is . . .

2. Topics for Session One

WHAT Do Children Need to Learn?

a. Hand out a copy of "Personal Skills a Child Needs to Learn" for each child represented. Note that this class is about "skills," not merely chores.

b. For discussion: Some classes have added making beds, caring for pets, shoveling snow. What other skills would your class add?

c. Exercise: Take time for parents to mark which skills each child already knows.

WHY Do They Need to Learn?

a. Read aloud page 15 and the first two lines of page 16.

b. For discussion: From the box on page 181 (condensed from Chapter 1), which reasons do you feel are most important for teaching household skills? Are there other reasons as well?

Why Do WE Need to Teach Them?

For discussion: In terms of teaching personal skills and a work ethic, how is this generation of parents different from previous ones? What roles and responsibilities are given to—or left to—parents?

3. Closing

Tell or read the mockingbird story on page 16. Ask God's blessing on each family by name.

ASSIGNMENTS

1. Read Chapters 3 and 4 for next week.

2. Practice:

   For children under 7: Consider the age-appropriate skills on page 87 and note which your child can already do. Choose one new skill to teach. (See "How to Teach a Child a Skill," page 80.) Practice the skill several times this week.

For children over 7: Go over the Skills List together. Mark what the child can already do. If you question a skill, ask your child to demonstrate it. If mastered, accept it. If not, refine it a bit. Let each child choose one new skill to learn, and teach it during the week. (See "How to Teach a Child a Skill," page 80.)

Why a Child Needs to Learn Household Skills

To learn to care for his or her own personal needs.

To learn to serve on a "family team," which
a. enables the family to do housework in less time
b. releases time for other activities
c. teaches decision making, evaluation, and problem solving
d. develops skills, initiative, competence, and self-esteem
e. instills a sense that the family is a priority
f. teaches that housework belongs to everyone

To learn that serving others is important.

To develop a work ethic and a sense of responsibility
a. when work is hard, nasty, or boring
b. when we would rather do something else
c. because other people are counting on us to do our share

To learn to care for the world.

Session Two

WHY DON'T WE TEACH THEM?

BASED ON CHAPTERS THREE AND FOUR

LEADER ADVANCE PREPARATION

Read Chapters 3 and 4 of this book and become familiar with the suggested session outline below.

SUGGESTED SESSION OUTLINE

1. Beginning

Prayer. Affirm your intent as parents to seek what is best for your children, even if it sometimes means letting God change you.

Welcome. Ask new group members to introduce themselves and tell something about their children. Ask former group members to describe experiences of teaching new skills in the past week.

Recap. Review again the box from last week's lesson, "Why a Child Needs to Learn Household Skills."

2. Topics for Session Two

Personal Parenting Styles

a. Go over the box on the following page (condensed from Chapter 3).

b. For discussion: Parents "train" a child during potty training. Do parents use any of these excuses as a reason not to potty train? Why not? How might the experience of potty training help parents overcome personal styles that prevent them from teaching household skills as well?

Personal Parenting Styles

Perfectionist: *"I like things done RIGHT—which means MY way."*

Servant: *"I like to do things FOR my children."*

Saint: *"Childhood is too short to waste it on housework."*

Martyr: *"They see how much I do. They ought to volunteer to help me."*

Compensator: *"My poor child has been through so much, I hate to add the burden of housework."*

Shield: *"I don't want my child to have to do all the tough things I had to do as a child."*

Dynamo: *"I've organized my housework so I can do it efficiently and fast. Teaching children to do it, and making them do it, takes more time than doing it myself."*

Abdicator: *"Making a child do housework is just too much hassle."*

Privileged parent: *"We have servants. Why should children do servants' work?"*

Sloth: *"I frankly don't care what my kids do, so long as they don't bother me."*

---

c. Exercise: Individually, circle personal parenting style(s)—one or more. Then complete the sentence below.

    Personal Parenting Statement of Commitment: *In order to commit myself to teaching my child(ren) household responsibilities, I need to change my behavior in the following way(s):*

d. For discussion: Is there anything from the exercise someone is willing to share?

Differences Between Two Parents' Parenting Styles

a. Point out that different upbringings often make spouses differ on questions like "How clean is 'clean'?" and "How often do we need to clean?"

b. Exercise: As a group, take the quiz "How Much Do You Know?" on page 51.

c. For discussion: In your own households, how have differences in parents' upbringing been a barrier to teaching children household responsibilities? How have you gotten beyond those differences? For remaining barriers, what can others in the group suggest—from Chapter 4 or personal experience?

3. Closing

Take a moment to silently reread commitment statements and pray for God's help in living up to those commitments during the coming week.

ASSIGNMENTS

1. Read Chapters 7 and 8 for next week.
2. Practice:

Choose one new skill per child and teach it this week.

Take steps to begin to practice whatever you have just committed yourself to do.

Session Three

WHAT DO WE TEACH, AND HOW?

BASED ON CHAPTERS SEVEN AND EIGHT

LEADER ADVANCE PREPARATION

Read Chapters 7 and 8 of this book and become familiar with the suggested session outline below. Think of one time in your life when you had to learn something new. Be prepared to tell about it briefly, if it's needed to stimulate class discussion.

SUGGESTED SESSION OUTLINE

1. **Beginning**

   Prayer. Ask for new insight on how to teach your children what they need to know.

   Welcome. Ask new class members to tell about themselves and their children, and invite others to tell *briefly* about their experience in teaching new skills or adjusting their parenting styles in the past week. (Don't let this consume the hour!)

2. **Topics for Session Three**

   ### Age Appropriate Skills

   Look at lists on pages 87 and 91. Note:

   a. Each list is for a range of ages. Some skills are too difficult for the youngest members of each age range.

   b. "Skills" for two- and three-year-olds don't really help the parent, but merely provide a way for a child to work beside the parent. By the time a child is four, however, the tasks are genuinely needed by a family team and are skills a child needs to know.

How to Teach a Skill

a. Exercise: Remember a time when you had to learn a new thing. How did you learn it? (Leader may need to begin, in order to spark others' memories.)

b. For discussion: What helps us, as adults, learn something new?

c. Look at "How to Teach a Child a Skill" on page 80 and read aloud "What Kids Hate" below. Note that children learn the same way adults do: by being told, shown, allowed to try it, supervised, and allowed to fail and try again.

What Kids Hate

"I hate having my mom or dad add to a job after I thought I did it. For instance, they say, 'Wash the dishes.' Then, an hour later, they come back in and say 'Why didn't you wipe off the counters and put away the food?' They didn't tell me that was part of the job."

---

d. Exercise: Ask for two volunteers to teach the class how to wash dishes. Afterwards, as a group, critique their teaching. What did they do well? Not so well? Did they teach the *entire process* from start to finish?

e. Recap: When teaching, teach skills, not chores; teach skills appropriate to the age and ability of that particular child; and teach complete skills.

How to Make Teaching Easier

Exercise: Assign the following to different members of the group to read and briefly share with the entire class:

Tips to Help Preschoolers Learn (page 88)
Tips to Help Preschoolers Learn, continued (page 89)
Have materials in an appropriate size (page 78)
Work alongside a child (page 80)
Advance from the simple to the difficult (page 81)
Teach safety as you teach responsibility (page 82)
Never redo a job a child has done (page 82)

How to Make Cleaning More Fun

a. Point out games under "I'd Rather Be Playing" (pages 105–109).
b. For discussion: What has worked for families in the class to make learning easier and cleaning more fun?

3. Closing

Close with prayer for each family in the class.

ASSIGNMENTS

1. Read Chapter 5 for next week.
2. Practice: Try one of the cleaning games from Chapter 8 in your family this week.

Session Four

FAMILY MEETINGS

BASED ON CHAPTER FIVE

LEADER ADVANCE PREPARATION

Read Chapter 5 and become familiar with the suggested session outline below. Ask four or five class members to do the role playing for the group. Assign parts ahead of time so members can study their roles and not start out cold.

SUGGESTED SESSION OUTLINE

1. *Beginning*

Prayer. Thank God together for setting us in families and for giving us the families we have. Pray for wisdom to become a team that supports and nurtures one another.

Welcome. Meet new class members. Ask former class members to share how their cleaning games went this week, or their progress in teaching household skills at home.

Recap. So far the class has learned:

a. Children need to learn skills to care for themselves and the world around them, to learn to serve others, and to learn to be part of a family.

b. Children can often do more than we expect them to do at a given age.

c. Household skills have to be taught; they are not instinctively learned.

2. Topics for Session Four

Introducing the Family Meeting Concept

a. How many families in the group already have family meetings? Ask any who do to describe what happens and how they are structured. Do they deal just with chores or with other family concerns? How often are meetings held?

b. For discussion: The box "Why Have a Family Meeting?" gives some reasons for meeting together. What value can you see in holding meetings in your own families? What resistances would you run into? How could they be overcome?

What Does a Family Meeting Look Like?

a. Role-play a family meeting (10–15 minutes).

Mother: Believes that hers is the only correct way to clean. However, she is convinced that her children need to learn

---

Why Have a Family Meeting?

1. *To stay in touch as a family*: Celebrate and commiserate together, hear and deal with gripes before they fester, compare schedules, and put upcoming events on the family calendar.
2. *To teach how much work is needed to run a family, and plan chore schedules for a specific span of time*: List what has to be done, assign or choose tasks, set up a schedule, and decide what new skills need to be taught and when.
3. *To teach evaluation, system analysis, and problem solving*: Evaluate a previous schedule and assignments, retool parts that aren't working, or create a new plan.
4. *To teach that failure is a chance to reevaluate and move forward.*
5. *To teach that each of us can help others*: Solve problems together and give everyone a say in decisions, evaluations, and creating new plans.

household skills (done her way) and she's also over-whelmed by all she has to do. Prepare ahead by making a list of everything that needs to be done and by reading pages 68–70 to give you some ideas of what to say.

Father: Believes housework is women's work, except he is also willing to wash dishes, which he does very well. Otherwise, he feels that earning the living is his share in family responsibilities. However, he is willing to support his wife in getting the children to help around the house. His preferred method of doing that is for someone (himself) to tell them what they are to do each week. Prepare ahead by reading "I Have Too Much To Do" and "It's Your Job" on page 69.

First child: Very involved in music lessons, sports, and school. Doesn't want to do housework at all. Prepare ahead by reading "I Can't" on pages 68–69.

Second child: Doesn't mind doing housework, but has own ideas about when and how it ought to be done, and resents being told, rather than asked, to do it.

Situation: A very first family meeting. Mother has called the meeting to present her list of everything that needs to be done to keep the house running smoothly, to ask for help with housework, and to convince the others that the children need to learn household skills. Play out the situation based on how you think your own families would act.

b. For discussion: In what ways was this realistic? Unrealistic? What did the family accomplish? How might they have accomplished more? How might we use family meetings in our own homes?

3. Closing

Thank your local actors.

Pray for each family by name as you seek to become family teams and teach children what they need to know to become mature adults.

ASSIGNMENTS

1. Read Chapter 9 and reread "A Room of One's Own" on page 95 and "Defusing General Resistance" on page 70.
2. Practice: Hold a family meeting, if you think your family is ready for one.

Session Five

DEALING WITH RESISTANCE AND REBELLION

BASED ON CHAPTER NINE

LEADER'S ADVANCE PREPARATION

Read Chapter 9, reread "A Room of One's Own" on page 95 and "Defusing General Resistance" on page 70, and become familiar with the suggested session outline below. Prepare slips of paper with one of the following on each:

"It's my room, and I'll clean it if I want to."

"Why should I have to clean? Nobody else I know does."

"I don't mind dusting and vacuuming, but cleaning bathrooms? Yuck!"

"Why do I have to do that right now? Why can't I do it when I want to?"

"Okay, so I forgot my chores. I can't remember *everything!*"

SUGGESTED SESSION OUTLINE

1. Beginning

Prayer. Ask that as parents you may have grace, wisdom, and a sense of humor to deal with resistant or rebellious children.

Welcome. Introduce newcomers. Ask group members to report on any progress their families have made in teaching household skills this past week.

2. Topics for Session Five

Resistance of Many Sorts

a. Exercise: Hand out the prepared slips of paper and ask those who get one to read it and suggest how they would respond to that statement from a child. Let the group also contribute suggestions. Bring out suggestions from the book as well.

b. For discussion: (may limit time on each, or choose two or three to discuss)

1. Children, like adults, have differing personality types, schedule preferences, work paces, and ways of doing things. In what ways can families take that into account when setting up work schedules, and when do personality differences need to be submitted to family need?

2. Look at "Tips to Help Procrastinators" on page 117. How can a parent tell whether procrastination is silent rebellion or a silent plea for help with a task that seems too big or difficult?

3. What success have different families had with chore charts? Do family meetings and chore charts really help defuse resistance and cut down on nagging?

4. Ephesians 6:4 says that parents should not provoke their children to wrath, yet children often get provoked when parents insist that they do housework. One parent reminded her child that he had also objected to being potty trained, then asked, "Aren't you glad now I insisted?" as a prelude to talking about why learning household skills is equally important. How else can a parent who is convinced that the child needs to learn household skills defuse some of a child's anger?

5. Page 115 describes a "fairness approach" to solving conflicts. How might this work in your house, especially on the housework issue?

A Room of One's Own

For discussion: On page 95, the author suggests that the issue of cleaning a child's room may center not so much on cleanliness as on a power struggle between parent and child for "rights" to that space. On page 96, she lists several ways parents try to get children to clean the child's room.

1. How effective is each? What is the drawback to each? Do group members have other solutions?
2. Her implied conclusion is that how well a child cleans his or her own room is not necessarily a model for how the child will keep house as an adult *if* the child has learned household skills elsewhere in the house. What do you think about that?

3. Closing

Pray for wisdom as parents to listen to children to try to understand where anger and rebellion are coming from, and for courage to deal with it in a godly manner.

ASSIGNMENT

1. Read Chapters 10, 11, and 14.
2. Practice: Try dealing with resistance or rebellion in new ways this week. Discuss with your child how he or she feels about cleaning his or her own room—as opposed to cleaning shared parts of the house. Try to really listen. Work together toward a compromise you can both live with.

Session Six

CONSEQUENCES AND REWARDS

BASED ON CHAPTERS TEN, ELEVEN, AND FOURTEEN

LEADER ADVANCE PREPARATION

Read Chapters 10, 11, and 14 and become familiar with the suggested session outline below. Practice reading aloud from "What Happens If We Don't?" on page 161, or ask a good reader to prepare to read it as the class conclusion.

SUGGESTED SESSION OUTLINE

1. Beginning

Prayer. Thank God for your children; thank him also that each family is different, a lab in which we can learn to love, succeed, fail, and try again.

Welcome. Introduce any new members. Ask for reports from other group members on new ways they dealt with resistance last week, or on successes in teaching new skills.

2. Topics for Session Six

Teaching by Consequences

a. For discussion: Some experts say that children learn far more from natural than from related or imposed consequences. Why might this be true? (See the box on page 196.)

b. Exercise: Suggest one natural and one related consequence for the following:

    1. A family member fails to cook on an assigned night, throwing off the entire family's evening schedule.

    2. The person scheduled to do the family laundry fails to complete the laundry before it's needed.

    3. A family member mops the kitchen, but does a poor job and, leaving the bucket of water in the middle of the floor, goes to a friend's house for the night.

c. For discussion: What natural consequences can the group think of for other common household infractions? What personal resistances do parents have to overcome to permit children to suffer natural consequences?

Three Kinds of Consequences

Natural Consequences: A direct result of actions. (*Example*: If you don't take your dishes to the sink, you will eat on those dishes the next meal here.)

Related Consequences: Connected to actions in a recognizable way. (*Example*: If you don't take your dishes to the sink, you will wash dishes for the next family meal.)

Imposed Consequences: A punishment chosen by authority, unrelated to actions. (*Example*: If you don't take your dishes to the sink, you can't play with your friends.)

Praising Children for Work

a. The book lists four kinds of praise that may not be rewarding for a child:

    1. Too much praise or praise for mediocre performance.

    2. Praise that sets up the parent as the final authority on what is a "good" job.

    3. Praise for jobs that anyone can do well.

    4. Praise for doing something the child already finds rewarding.

b. For discussion: Why might those types of praise be ineffective or even harmful to a child's self-esteem? What kinds of praise are more effective? Why? (Hint: see pages 133–34).

Rewarding Children for Work

a. Exercise: Ask group members to remember how they were rewarded for work as children. Also name various ways families have rewarded their own children.

b. For discussion: What rewards—besides money—can be important to a child?

c. Exercise: Individually mark the scale below, then compare to see where this group comes out on the Pay for Work Continuum.

d. For discussion: Each family is different, and each family goes through different stages (such as ages, income levels, and needs). How much flexibility does a family need in order to deal with various stages? What problems are families in your group having in setting appropriate rewards? What wisdom can the group offer them?

Pay for Work Continuum

Some "experts" advise paying children for *all* tasks, since adults work for pay and the only work children can do is at home. Other experts are adamant that a child should *never* be paid for working at home, since that work is done on behalf of the family and adults don't get paid for cooking, dishes, laundry, etc. Where would you put yourself in that debate? Put an X on the line closest to where you and your family are at this point:

ALWAYS pay   NEVER pay
children for work   children for work

---

3. *Conclusion*

a. Exercise: This class has covered many topics. Look back at your expectations, as expressed in Session One. In what ways did the class meet your expectations? What has been of value for you and your family? What changes have you made or do you plan to make?

b. Read aloud: "The Courage Not to Be Perfect" on pages 163–65.

c. Pray for all the families in this group as you conclude the class.

ASSIGNMENT

Practice: Try teaching more lessons through deliberate use of natural consequences this week. Discuss as a family what rewards seem appropriate at this stage in your family history for various types of work. Start praying together for your family team!

Notes

Notes

Notes

Notes

Notes

Also from Patricia Sprinkle . . .

Women Who Do Too Much is written for all women who are doing too much and know it. With wisdom and insight, Patricia Sprinkle provides guidelines and practical suggestions to help you move from a stress-filled life toward effective living. By learning how to set realistic goals, to do what is important (not merely urgent), and to develop your unique abilities, you can become the woman you were made to be.

Softcover ISBN: 0-310-53771-1
Mass Market ISBN: 0-310-21515-3

Women Home Alone is an upbeat, hands-on guide for self-sufficiency. In this insightful book, Patricia Sprinkle offers women—single, divorced, widowed, or married to a husband who travels often—the knowledge of police officers, mechanics, carpenters, financial advisers, and other professionals. She shares a wealth of information on topics such as making your home secure, planning for your financial future, coping with house repairs, and many, many more. With inspiration, humor, and a reminder of God's protection, *Women Home Alone* will help you enjoy the independence of being on your own.

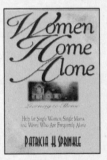

Softcover
ISBN: 0-310-20183-7

A Gift from God, formerly titled *In God's Image*, shows busy new mothers how babies teach us far more about God than we teach them. With 31 heartwarming and insightful meditations, Patricia Sprinkle takes a new mother from pregnancy to the time of birth up to her baby's first birthday. And with each stage of a baby's development, a mother will learn more about God, who created her baby in his own image. *A Gift from God* will be spiritual nourishment for a new mother's soul.

Hardcover
ISBN: 0-310-41080-0

ZondervanPublishingHouse
Grand Rapids, Michigan

A Division of HarperCollins*Publishers*

Author Seminars

Women Who Do Too Much Seminar

A workshop for women who know they are doing too much but don't know how to stop.

Today's woman is always busy, but seldom feels she gets enough done. She sets goals for herself, but gets so swamped meeting other people's needs that she fails to accomplish her own goals. Whether you are married or single, employed or at home, this workshop challenges every woman frazzled by trying to juggle too many roles to prayerfully seek God's plan for her life and get rid of hindrances to that plan.

Children Who Do Too Little Seminar

A workshop for concerned parents who know children need to learn household skills, but don't know how to begin.

Today's children are bright and busy people. So why, when they grow up, do so many of them have problems getting a job, holding a job, and staying married? Today's parents are bright and busy people. So why are they exhausting themselves doing all the housework and driving the children all over town? This workshop is designed for parents or entire families to help prepare children for responsible adulthood.

For more information, contact
Patricia Sprinkle
15086 SW 113th Street
Miami, FL 33196
305-385-3818

We want to hear from you. Please send your comments about this
book to us in care of the address below. Thank you.

ZondervanPublishingHouse
Grand Rapids, Michigan 49530
http://www.zondervan.com